Praise for
"YOU DON'T HAVE TO GO HOME FROM WORK EXHAUSTED!"

❝*Move over, Albert Einstein. Ann McGee-Cooper has an updated formula: Energy equals work plus play.* **❞**

Chicago Tribune

❝*There are few books that have the power to change the way you work or the way you live. This book may be one of them. If you ever feel that your work life leaves you tired—either physically, intellectually, or spiritually—this is definitely a book for you.* **❞**

Behavioral Sciences Newsletter

❝*Stress Detectives—Ann McGee-Cooper and Duane Trammell help employers recognize the symptoms of stress, depression, and burnout in their employees.* **❞**

USA Today

❝*If you've been dragging home from work too tired to get an interesting dinner on the table or help the kids with their homework and can't plan a vacation or a weekend because nothing sounds fun anymore, this book can help.* **❞**

The Seattle Times

YOU DON'T HAVE TO GO HOME FROM WORK EXHAUSTED!

A Program to Bring Joy, Energy, and Balance to Your Life

BY

ANN MCGEE-COOPER

WITH

DUANE TRAMMELL & BARBARA LAU

BANTAM BOOKS
NEW YORK · TORONTO · LONDON · SYDNEY · AUCKLAND

YOU DON'T HAVE TO GO HOME FROM WORK EXHAUSTED!
A Bantam Book/published by arrangement with the authors

PRINTING HISTORY
Bowen & Rogers edition published 1990
Bantam edition / October 1992

ISBN 0-553-37061-8

Published simultaneously in the United States and Canada

Bantam Books are published by Bantam Books, a division of Bantam
Doubleday Dell Publishing Group, Inc. Its trademark, consisting of the
words "Bantam Books" and the portrayal of a rooster, is Registered in
U.S. Patent and Trademark Office and in other countries. Marca
Registrada. Bantam Books, 666 Fifth Avenue, New York, New York 10103.

PRINTED IN THE UNITED STATES OF AMERICA

0 9 8 7 6 5 4 3 2 1

CONTENTS

PART ONE

Tired of Being Tired?

PART TWO

Reclaiming KidSpirit

PART THREE

Putting Both Sides of Your Brain to Work

PART FOUR

Energy Traps and Solutions

CONTENTS

PART FIVE

Energy Engineering Strategies

DEDICATION

We dedicate this book to two masters of Energy Engineering. The first is Georgia Ulrich, who at age eighty-four enjoys a full-time career as a business partner with us, reads six to eight books per week both for fun and for our research, manages a household for three, enjoys daily exercise, and claims to have more fun than most people with a variety of hobbies and friends of all ages. To celebrate her eightieth birthday she went up in a hot-air balloon. She exemplifies through her actions the rich rewards of living life fully. When asked her secrets for staying so fully invested in living, Georgia shared these tips:

- hang on to your humor,
- don't ask for permission, just do it! and
- make everything fun.

The second great inspiring Energy Engineering role model is Bob Gary, executive vice president, TU Electric, Generation. For the past six years we have watched him turn problems into opportunities as he has coached us and several hundred others in applying the secrets of brain integration to our daily lives. We would gather and synthesize the research and he would show us how powerful it can be by putting it to work in real situations. Bob has literally saved lives with his intuitive genius and, with his whole-brained team, has turned impossible situations into innovative business wins. On weekends you can usually find him having a grand time on his farm with his wife Joyce and his grandchildren. A master of play and mischief, Bob personifies the genius of abundant energy, innovation, and servant leadership.

PREFACE:

How Energy Engineering Was Born

After writing *Time Management for Unmanageable People,* Duane Trammell and I realized that finding enough time in the day just wasn't enough. Another major challenge was finding enough energy to keep working—*and* relaxing *and* playing—at 3:00 P.M., 6:00 P.M., 9:00 P.M., and so on. We found, for instance, that we could teach our clients how to budget time for a big project at 2:00 P.M. But if they didn't have a good reserve of energy stored up, the project either dragged on forever or was done in a mediocre fashion.

Our clients complained of needing more energy for these activities:

- putting in a truly productive and creative eight to ten hours on the job day after day;

- doing more than flopping on the couch and watching mindless TV sitcoms at night;

- developing new interests and activities in their spare time;

- taking up a physical activity or sport; and

- spending quality time with family and friends on the weekend.

Without abundant energy, these things rarely seem to get accomplished. Or we do them half-heartedly, merely going through the motions, so that the satisfaction we could derive from them is greatly diminished.

Our team at Ann McGee-Cooper and Associates, Inc., in Dallas decided to study *how to maintain and maximize one's energy, productivity, and overall zest for life each day of the year.* As we began our research, we discovered that very little had been written on the subject. A profusion of material on stress management, however, had flooded the market over the past ten years. Although stress can definitely be a factor in low energy, getting stress under control does not necessarily result in sustained high energy levels and increased motivation. In fact, managing stress and maximizing energy are two different functions, with separate solutions and problems.

In addition to collecting whatever data we could find on factors contributing to low and high energy, we interviewed many of our clients on the topic. Then we tested our ideas on ourselves, our friends, and interested clients. During the course of our research we also looked at four key populations:

1. highly successful executives who manage to get a tremendous amount of work done while enjoying a full range of outside activities;

2. people recognized as geniuses—inventors, scientists, artists, and others who were very productive and creative throughout their lives, even into their seventies and eighties;

3. preschool children, perhaps the most energetic population of all, who seem to have an inexhaustible supply of energy; and

4. self-actualized people as defined by the research of Abraham Maslow.

We searched out patterns these several groups held in common and were both surprised and delighted to discover several significant new insights regarding strategies adults can learn to recreate the abundant energy of small children. At first we set about seeing whether our discovery would generate more energy for ourselves, our team, and our families. The success rate was unusually high, so in 1984 we designed these strategies into a two-day Energy Engineering seminar that we took "on the road." We crisscrossed the country teaching these concepts to hundreds of very diverse groups: educators, Junior League members, health care professionals, dozens of corporations, and government agencies. The response was enthusiastic, so we looked for a way to study the long-term outcomes of these strategies in greater depth.

As a result, we shifted our research efforts. For the past six years we have worked almost exclusively with two large corporate groups, Texas Utilities and Fluor Daniel, Inc.

Fluor Daniel, Fluor Corporation's principal operating business unit, has been recognized as the number one contractor for the fourth year in a row by the *Engineering News-Record*. It provides global capability from more than fifty offices located around the world through the teamwork of over 40,000 people. The principal subsidiary of Texas Utilities is TU Electric, which provides electricity to a service area populated by more than five million people—about one-third of the population of the state of Texas, including the Dallas–Fort Worth Metroplex. In 1991, TU Electric ranked number one nationally in kilowatt-hour sales.There are more than 15,000 employees in the Texas Utilities system.

To date, nearly 3,000 corporate leaders as well as their direct reports and spouses have participated in Energy Engineering programs. In addition, hundreds of employees in Texas Utilities and representatives from Fluor Daniel, Bechtel, Westinghouse, Stone & Webster, Brown & Root, and Impell have become involved in testing and applying our energy strategies.

And what is their assessment of our ideas? Top executives who already were operating at a commendable energy level subjectively rated their energy increase at an average of 40 percent on our follow-up evaluations. Several executives reported a 100 percent energy boost! And people who were struggling to balance their careers and family responsibilities have been extremely enthusiastic as well. Thus we know these energy strategies work for lots of different people in lots of different ways.

Ann McGee-Cooper
July 1, 1992

ACKNOWLEDGMENTS

Although we three had the fun of writing the book, we have many to thank for making this vision a reality. Our business partners Carolyn Benard, Diane Bullard Cory, Jonnie Haug, Marybeth Hoesterey, Anna Irving, Janet Kirby, Rayo McCollough, Mike Mann, Jackie Maxwell, Karol Omlor, Kay Russell, Billie Snider, and Georgia Ulrich have all been active members of the research, development, and production process. No one could ever imagine the dedication, energy, and imagination they brought to this task.

We found a marvelous team to produce the book, headed by Ray Bard. They include:

Suzanne Pustejovsky	art director, text/cover design
Helen Hyams	copyeditor
Michael Donahue	marketing consultant
Mike Krone	illustrator
Judy Barrett	writer

We thank them for bringing their professional polish to the project and for agreeing to break lots of rules.

Our families have been patient and supportive as we have involved them in all sorts of crazy, fun, and innovative experiments in our search to learn the secrets of whole-brained energy.

Perhaps our greatest debt is to our clients over the past seven years who have participated in Energy Engineering seminars and given us generous feedback on what worked for them, and how and why it did. Much of the material in this book belongs to these pioneers, their families, and their learning partners who taught us through their lives, imaginative leadership, and creative sharing.

INTRODUCTION:

Learning Energy Engineering the Hard Way

by Ann McGee-Cooper

I grew up with two distinct role models for Energy Engineering. My dad used the typical business model: work hard, go to the office early, stay late, come home exhausted, always meet deadlines, and so on. We took annual vacations and did fun things together, but I remember that he spent most of his evenings just being tired, listening to the radio, and going to sleep in his big easy chair. My mom, on the other hand, had a different energy style. To this day, she gets more work done than anyone I have ever been around and she has more fun in the process! She has always been a master at finding ways to meet two goals with one effort, and she knows how to recruit others to assist her. She has lots of interests, gets plenty of exercise, has a great sense of humor, and at the age of eighty-four works at a full-time career while running a household for three people! She also enjoys a wide range of friends of all ages, reads several books a week, and keeps us all entertained with her ideas and new things she is learning.

So you can see why it came naturally for me to grow up expecting to work hard and accomplish many things at once. When I was young, I picked up my father's work patterns by keeping busy in all my after-school hours with small jobs, extracurricular activities, and summer jobs to help pay for college. In addition, while in high school I earned a scholarship to museum classes and completed the equivalent of a university program in art by the time I graduated from high school. To compound my work load, I was dyslexic (which I did not discover until I was much older). This forced me to do more schoolwork in order to keep up and make good grades. Thus, working hard was an everyday phenomenon to me.

Then in college I filled every waking hour with a heavy course load, volunteer work, and college organizations. When I graduated with a B.S. in design and a minor in architecture from The University of Texas at Austin, I immediately married and put my husband through Drew Seminary while teaching grade school plus museum art classes on Saturdays. It was not unusual for me to have four jobs going at once while I supported the family and raised my son.

Next came graduate school with an M.F.A. at Southern Methodist University, then an Ed.D. from Columbia by commuting between Dallas and New York and finishing with highest honors earned in record time. This was a very fertile time for me as I continued my thirty-five years of research in the areas of creativity and began to explore brain hemisphericity. My doctoral project was to develop a Teacher Survival Program. It was based on my observation that often the most creative young teachers become targets of the system and drop out, frustrated and drained of their creative energy. I decided to study this pattern and see whether I could develop a support system to help these creative change agents stay effective and happy within the demands of their job.

I designed a dual program of studying creative problem solving along with the more specific challenges facing the teachers. Another motivating element built into my doctoral work was my meetings with Margaret Mead. We met several times to review my research and to apply valuable insights from her own findings.

I poured all of my energy into my academic work and my very demanding job, taking it for granted that I would have to forgo fun times during this period of my life. But once the pattern was set, I seemed unable to break out of it. Playing "Superwoman" as a single mother, full-time college instructor at SMU, part-time business consultant, and active volunteer, I went seven years without taking more than an occasional weekend off. I established the Experimental Arts Program at SMU and supervised its growth into an internationally recognized project involving 5,500 teachers, students, and parents.

My involvement in all of these areas provides the groundwork for many of the ideas presented in this book. But I had not yet learned how to balance and sustain my energy reserves. Finally I developed a serious case of burnout and had a major problem that required surgery. I realized that life was controlling me more than I was controlling life.

So I took a one-year sabbatical to rethink my life, my priorities, and my use of time. After taking stock of my goals and the advice of some special mentors, I began to restructure my work and leisure time from scratch. I said good-bye and good riddance to some exhausting work habits and behavior traits. Around eleven years ago I remarried and tried a new weekly work schedule that my husband, a dentist, uses with great success. He sees patients three and one-half days a week. Then he goes into "retirement" the rest of the week, using that time to pursue his outside interests and renew his energy. During the years I experimented with that schedule, I found that I was producing more than I had previously because on the days I worked, I felt utterly refreshed, creative, and motivated. Although my work and travel schedule has again expanded to a five-day work week, I still integrate work with periods of play and recreation, and I try to keep weekends free for family, fun, and personal growth.

Experiencing the benefits of these new work- and lifestyles made me want to encourage others to seek a better balance between work and play. The writing of this book represents a synthesis of many aspects of my life and work: doctoral studies, ongoing research on brain dominance and learning methods, development programs with corporate leaders, seminars with a wide range of professionals, fieldwork with major companies, and, finally, my own experiences in balancing career goals with personal needs.

Creating a Shared Vision

I met Duane Trammell, my managing partner, at a seminar I developed for teachers who were in danger of burnout. Duane had been given thirty-eight students performing three grade levels below their age in an urban area with all its related problems. I shared with him some ideas on how to take time out for himself, renew his own energy through play, and then use some creative energy strategies with his students. We shared ideas back and forth with each other for five years, and the next thing I knew, he was winning the Ross Perot Award for Excellence in Teaching. In 1984, we collaborated on several projects, one of which was Energy Engineering; this was the beginning of our partnership. We began to share a vision of a creative new business that could help educators, business leaders, and people in all walks of life learn to tap the unlimited potential that leads to heightened creativity and abundant energy. Within two years we had developed enough business to support Duane's move into our full-time consulting business.

Several years later, Barbara Lau, a bright young freelance writer, called to learn more about our innovative approach. We had expanded well beyond traditional time management to considering the whole brain. Barbara attended several seminars, investigated how thoroughly we used what we taught in our own lives, and soon was totally immersed, bringing her own fresh insights. She wrote several articles for major publications about our work, with each article becoming more knowledgeable. When we decided to write this book, we knew we wanted Barbara's help. She would be far more than a gifted writer, for she had taught us a great deal from her own perspective as a working mom with a baby girl, a husband in graduate school, and a full-time career teaching seminars and writing.

We discovered after tracking the needs of business and community leaders, homemakers, educators, and health care professionals that creating and maintaining a high quality of energy was a top need all across the culture. These people weren't talking about getting from burnout back up to average energy. They were asking for help in creating the abundant, self-renewing energy that peak performers and winners in every field seem to maintain.

We began to see a completely new dimension emerge. All of our clients were investing in a cultural change focusing on quality, continuous improvement, productivity, safety, and teaming. As a result of these studies, we discovered that learning to "engineer," or understand and manage, your own energy and that of others is key to all these initiatives.

Furthermore, we learned that these changes can't exist only in the workplace. Whatever beliefs and behaviors we use at work seem to follow us home. If we are stressed, in conflict, and miserable at home, we go to work in pieces. If we are frustrated and overwhelmed at work, the frustration follows us home. So, with the support and encouragement of the corporate leaders who were our clients, we involved spouses, family, and significant others in our process.

The results continue to be amazing. Together we have learned that you can't achieve any of the above goals without learning to have fun, lighten up, and develop trust and interdependence on the job and at home. When we attempt to achieve these goals of quality, productivity, improved safety, and excellence by pushing harder and longer, we push ourselves and each other right into burnout!

The fact that the stakes are so high and the pressure so great makes complacency no longer an option. It demands that we make some changes now. We cannot prosper until or unless our beliefs, traditions, and habits change dramatically. By learning to become healthier, more caring, more interdependent, responsible, and creative people, all of our goals and dreams can be realized. And along the way, each day can be balanced, productive, fun, and fulfilling. Urgency and looming problems become our friends, leveraging us faster into changes we already needed to make, whether we recognized it or not. If we can think of the complex pressures, problems, and demands on our lives as a wake-up call, there are many very positive and productive options waiting to be discovered.

Prepare for a life-changing journey. It has been that for all of us. A tremendous increase in energy every year has not been unusual. If you keep adding energy and compounding it, abundant, growing energy becomes easily possible!

ENERGY MYTHS:

Fables That Foil Our Energy

❝ I do not know what I may appear to the world; but to myself I seem to have been only like a boy playing on the seashore, and diverting myself in now and then finding a smoother pebble or a prettier shell than ordinary, whilst the great ocean of truth lay all undiscovered before me. ❞

—Sir Isaac Newton,
Brewster's Memories of Newton

❝ Each thought becomes an anxiety in my brain. I am becoming the ugliest of all things: a busy man. ❞
—André Gide

You don't have to go home from work every day feeling tired and exhausted. Through creative Energy Engineering, you can bring vitality and enthusiasm to your evenings and weekends as well. But you must begin by unlearning some comfortable habits that are unproductive and that drain you of precious energy.

At our seminars, we often tell a story that is popular among those who teach creativity. It describes a professor who visits a Japanese Zen master. The wise teacher immediately sees that the professor is rather set in his ways and needs to be taught a vital lesson. The master picks up a pot of tea and begins filling the man's outheld cup. He fills the cup to overflowing, tranquilly watching the tea spill out of the saucer onto the table and floor. "Master!" shouts the student in dismay. "Can't you see? My cup is already full. There is no room for more tea in it."

"Just like your head," replies the master. "If you wish to make room for new ideas, first you must empty your head of the old ideas that are blocking your mind."

This lesson serves as excellent advice for reading this book and reevaluating your own filled-to-the-brim cup of notions. For it is difficult to abandon "the way it's always been done before" in order to risk thinking and trying something new. But you must be open to this if you wish to change things for the better in your life.

Myth 1: Energy Can Only Be Restored by Sleep

Wrong! There are many ways to restore energy during the day and night, and sleeping is just one of them. Time spent exercising, playing, laughing, having fun, being creative, relaxing, meditating, and switching to other activities can also renew your momentum and increase alertness. And you can do these energy-building activities throughout the day rather than wait for bedtime to restore your energy. For instance, Albert Schweitzer and Thomas Edison—both notorious for having unusual sleep patterns—would play the organ and piano as a form of relaxation and stimulation. In *Genius in the Jungle,* a biography of Schweitzer, author Joseph Gollomb writes: "By that time a little sleep was even worse than none at all, as so often happens when one has overdrawn on one's reserves. He [Schweitzer] had to have something that would rest him more than sleep. At such times . . . he would climb to the organ loft and play."

Sometimes sleep can actually drain your energy more than restore it. If you fall asleep while you are experiencing anxiety, muscular tension, and exhaustion, stress toxins can remain in your body rather than being expelled through exercise and relaxing activities. This is often the case when people complain that they feel as if they "hardly slept a wink" or "fought a battle in their sleep." Moreover, it is a fallacy to assume that all people are at their maximum energy level upon waking up. Some people feel most energetic and alert at other times in the day.

The main point you should remember regarding this myth is that you are not like a car that starts off with a full tank in the morning but is destined to run out of gas after eight hours of driving. There are many techniques available to you for refueling your energy reserves a little bit at a time throughout the day.

Myth 2: We All Need Seven to Eight Hours of Sleep per Night

Wrong again! Although the majority of people seem to feel best with from six to eight hours of sleep each night, by no means is this a requirement for all people. Many of our most celebrated geniuses and other very active folks do well with much less sleep or unusual sleep patterns. For example, R. Buckminster Fuller's spontaneous sleep habits allowed him to work vigorously nearly around the clock. He would be actively engaged in work and play for about six hours. At that point he would usually feel drowsy, and wherever he was, he would lie down on the floor and sleep for about thirty minutes. Refreshed, he would wake up and start another six hours of intense activity, continuing this pattern throughout the day and night. That amounts to only two hours of sleep per day. Explained Fuller (as quoted in *Bucky* by Hugh Kenner): "I was trying to find out how much I could get done, and noticed that a dog, when he gets tired, simply lies down and sleeps. So it could be that if the minute you're tired you just lie down, you'd need far less sleep. So I just tried it out." Bucky called this "dymaxion sleep," *dymaxion* meaning doing more with less.

Don Frick, a self-employed writer and producer in Indianapolis, often breaks his sleep time into two to three intervals during a twenty-four-hour period. He explains: "I've found that I don't need eight hours of sleep at one stretch. If I just listen to the signals my body gives me, then there are naturally occurring times when my productivity is high and when it crashes. I'm no good after lunch, for example, so I've gotten into the habit of sleeping one and one-half hours after eating. Then I often work at nights, but around 3:30 A.M. there's absolutely no productive work left inside me. So I'll sleep until 6:00 or 7:30 A.M. I feel fine going on this way for about five days. Then my body gives me a cue, and I'll let myself sleep for a nine-hour shift, which totally revives me."

These examples are not meant to encourage you to attempt such shortened sleep patterns unless you feel they might work for you. Our main point is that these highly creative people listened to their internal voice when it told them they needed rest; they then found that they were able to jump back into high gear.

Many executives follow a modified version of these sleep patterns. Once or twice a day they have their secretaries block all interruptions while they stretch out on their office couch (or floor!) and take a fifteen- to thirty-minute nap. Others have a short deep-breathing or meditation session.

Daily aerobic exercise can also decrease the amount of sleep people require. Exercise provides some of the benefits of sleep by helping to release tension and stress toxins, thereby producing a feeling of relaxation and well-being. It also tends to produce deeper and less fitful sleep. Finally, many older people find that they need less sleep.

In fact, the importance of listening to and trusting what your body is telling you was another of our key insights. Each person's body seems to have its own unique way of working best. If we intuitively follow what it is requesting, an amazing new level of energy usually results.

Myth 3: Loss of Energy Is Part of the Aging Process

Wrong once again! Energy does not have to slowly burn out as we age, like a flame on a candlestick. Instead, our individual energy plateaus appear to be linked much more closely to our health and to our passionate involvement in our work and our life. Other fundamental factors include being in sync with our brain dominance; having energizing eating and exercising patterns; being involved in different projects; having a purpose in life; being curious about learning new things; spending time in playful, fun activities; and daring to dream dreams that really matter to us. Once again, many noteworthy people — Georgia O'Keeffe, Pablo Picasso, Thomas Edison, Albert Schweitzer, and R. Buckminster

Fuller, to name a few—continued to be productive and energetic beyond their ninetieth year. In addition, many business leaders we have worked with have maintained the vitality and spontaneity they had in their youth.

In the November 1988 issue of *Spirit! Magazine,* George Waldon reported that the late Sam Walton, the seventy-one-year-old founder of Wal-Mart who, according to *Forbes,* was the richest man in America, "vowed to do the hula on Wall Street if [his company] could tally up a net pretax profit of more than 8%." When the company did it, Sam "donned a grass skirt over his business suit . . . and shimmied along with some traditional Hawaiian dancers and musicians on the sidewalk in front of a downtown Manhattan office building."

Myth 4: The Main Source of Energy Is Physical Health

Wrong again! Although feeling healthy certainly contributes to your well-being and energy levels, you also need to be interested and engaged in life in order to want to be active in the first place! And two of the key elements that cause people to vigorously embrace life are having a strong purpose for living and having a commitment to reaching a certain goal.

Dr. Larry Dossey, former chief of staff at Medical City Dallas Hospital and a leading reformer of both traditional and holistic medicine, takes this idea even further. He believes that energy in his work comes from these two important sources:

1. A sense of purpose that goes beyond the details of "the job," whatever that might be. There must be a sense that what I do is somehow congruent with the overall purpose, design, and flow of the universe as I experience it—that my work fits with the Big Picture. I can't overemphasize the importance of this factor. I believe it is some sort of "megatrend"—the need to feel that one's work is somehow aligned with what's best for the earth itself. I would suggest that the energy drain many workers feel comes from a sense that they're not aligned with what's best for

the earth. This frequently leads to a feeling of malaise and emotional and spiritual poverty.

2. A sense of the "top line." This is opposed to the "bottom line," which we usually say is the ultimate criterion of the worth of our work. Great achievers have an abiding sense of what the top line is (a concern for people and quality of life), and it is one of the most energizing aspects of their lives. Psychologist Abraham Maslow interviewed great accomplishers to see what made them tick. He found that these high-energy people not only had a great concern for people and quality of life, but were dedicated to a purpose or mission for their life that gave them momentum.

It is unquestionably energizing to love your work. When Ben Bradlee, editor of the *Washington Post,* was asked if he would pursue the same career again, he answered: "I would do it so fast! I wonder what took me so long—I didn't start till I was sixteen, when I got my first job as a copy boy."

Passion will rejuvenate you in a deeper, more long-lasting way than simply getting enough sleep and feeling healthy. Harriet Beecher Stowe's *Uncle Tom's Cabin* rocked the world, but she was an unlikely literary giant. No one but her husband took her writing seriously. She worked at the kitchen table, writing on brown paper, surrounded by confusion and small children. She was poor, harried, not particularly healthy, and always pressed for time, but she felt passionately about the issue of slavery and vowed to tell the story. Although she expected to make no money from the book, the publication of *Uncle Tom's Cabin* proved to be a turning point in her life. It immediately made her a worldwide celebrity and provided her with the financial security to write for thirty more years and live comfortably for the first time in her forty-one years.

Along with passion, the most important and undergirding element of high-energy living seems to be balance. Learning to live in balance, allowing time for both work and a rewarding personal life, will bring synergy, joy, enthusiasm, and creativity to your life.

HOW PASSION AND DREAMS BEGET ENERGY:

Nothing Much Happens Without a Dream

❝ *We may affirm absolutely that nothing great in the world has been accomplished without passion.* **❞**
—**Georg Wilhelm Friedrich Hegel,** *Philosophy of History*

❝ *I now do energizing hobbies during the time after work that I used to spend just being tired.* **❞**
—**Ed Platt, Manager of Generation, Eastern Gas Plants, TU Electric**

❝ *Those who dream by day are cognizant of many things which escape those who dream only by night.* **❞**
—**Edgar Allan Poe, "Eleanora"**

s you search out people who can serve as role models of high and inspirational levels of energy, look for passion in their lives. We're not referring to sexual passion, though often a high level of sexuality seems to be part of the pattern. For some people, it's a person—a new friend, mate, grandchild, or acquaintance—that instills in their lives fresh vitality and meaning. For others, it's the blossoming of a new talent or interest, such as learning to ice skate at thirty-five, finally finding the "perfect job" at forty-five, restoring an old house at sixty, or going back to college at fifty to get that degree they never earned.

Live Outside the Bounds of What's Safe and Familiar

When we speak of passion, we are also referring to a general enthusiasm for life—for learning, for music, for government reform, and for whatever else might capture our interest and imagination. People of uniquely high energy seem to live outside the bounds of quiet interest. You may find them up at all hours, as when Edison stayed up for forty hours watching his first light bulb to be certain it didn't flicker.

Applying this description to yourself, stop and think, "When did I last feel passion? And what or who inspires my passion?" Did you ever notice that passion seems to be contagious within your life? When you were courting and madly in love, didn't the sky seem bluer and the flowers smell sweeter? If you fell in love all over again at the age of fifty, didn't you find yourself enjoying "foolish things" such as flying kites, buying fresh flowers, or taking a walk barefoot in the rain and discovering a new, abundant energy source within yourself?

The point is, when you allow the governor of self-control to be withdrawn so that you *begin to experience life again as you did as a child,* without the tight restrictions of how others might judge you, you live with greater energy. And the energy drawn from one part of your life will leak into other parts of your life. You begin to challenge worn-out rules and restrictions in other areas of your life that no longer seem as necessary and significant. You might also begin to wonder whether there isn't a more meaningful way for you to live.

Fresh Circumstances Can Add Energy and Passion to Life

For example, last week you may have given a typical cocktail party and been somewhat bored with the same polite conversations with the same people. So this week you become inspired to think of new possibilities for the next of such parties. These people aren't boring, but the unchallenged guidelines of the usual cocktail party may be. Instead, what if you threw a fantasy party and everyone came dressed as their fantasy career?

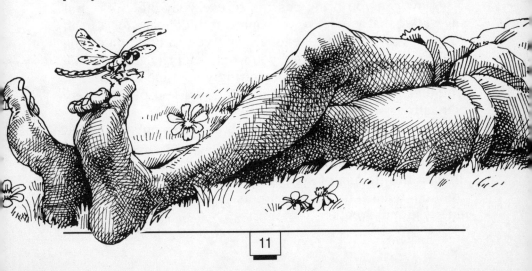

ACTION ITEM

Ask yourself: What are you passionate about? Where, or when, do you allow yourself to experience passion? If skepticism or cynicism has crept in, what could rekindle your passion? You might take a look at the price you are paying for these two qualities. Age and experience are not necessarily strangers to passion. Ben Franklin, Thomas Jefferson, Eleanor Roosevelt, Madame Curie, Lee Iacocca, and Georgia O'Keeffe all knew defeat and discouragement. Yet all were able to hang on to a sense of passion about those things that really mattered to them. Perhaps passion is linked to a degree of caring about something. And perhaps we learn to protect ourselves from disappointment and defeat by not caring too much and by not risking things that seem far out of reach. But if we sacrifice high energy, deep involvement, and making a difference in life, is the price of our apathy and indifference too great?

Or what if the party centered on childhood, with guests bringing a childhood game and pictures of themselves in their youth? Instead of only having people of the same general age and background, what if you invited people in a wide range of ages? What can you learn from the elderly? from young children? from teenagers? Think of what new energy might be unleashed with such a mixture of people and fun ideas.

How can you bring passion to everyday life? We're not suggesting that you leave your mate at middle age for a fresh young lover. But we are encouraging you to find something you care so much about that you would willingly give your life for it. (Since *something* is devouring your time and energy, wouldn't you rather it be something you feel passionately committed to?)

We had a gathering at a church one evening and invited all ages. Each family brought homemade ice cream for the close of the celebration. The group of about forty people was divided into teams of six persons each. There were young children, teenagers, young parents, middle-aged people, and elderly grandparents.

Each team was given a problem to solve, such as world hunger or air and water pollution. Then they were given art materials and ideas for ways to solve these problems through fantasy inventions, such as stuffing pantyhose with crushed newspaper and dressing them in odds and ends of clothes. Each group was challenged to create a working model to present to the group within forty-five minutes. On one team a distinguished surgeon worked feverishly with a ten-year-old to stitch up an agricultural engineer who would farm the oceans and develop hydrogardens. Another group, a banker in his sixties and a young mother in her early twenties, designed a sound-effects tape to accompany their space-age solution to overpopulation.

Many reported that they had misgivings about attending such an evening. They were already tired by the time 6:00 P.M. rolled around, and they weren't sure this was their "cup of tea" anyway. Yet by the time each invention was shared, complete with original poetry, lots of laughter, and the risking of creative ideas, plus ice cream and a worship service about the gift of creativity and the great resource of individual differences, each person left with a new sense of hope, renewal, dedication, and quality energy.

How Do We Lose Our Passion?

If we choose the safer route, to lower our goals and only hope for realistic, sure possibilities, we limit our lives to the mediocre and rob ourselves of the chance for a really big win and all the excitement that goes with it.

When we vote for the high road, we choose to risk experiencing big disappointments and great losses by investing heavily in dreams and goals. To live with great passion means to "bet the farm" on each day of life. Yet we find we have to reconfront this choice again and again. For often, without realizing it, we slip back into the comfort of not caring quite so much, not risking, dreaming realistic rather than innovative dreams, not adventuring forth. Life becomes safer (and this may be needed and appropriate for a time). But it lacks the depth, the challenge, the richness, and the vitality that we have grown to love and enjoy. If our passion has been lost, we need to discover ways to rekindle it.

Dreams for a High-Energy Future

The writer Robert Greenleaf has said, "Nothing much happens without a dream. For something really great to happen, it takes a really great dream." Greenleaf and others who have spent their lives studying leaders and leadership qualities have discovered that one characteristic these leaders hold in common is dreaming great dreams and sharing their visions with others.

What is your dream or vision for your life? Is it a practical, fairly easy dream to obtain, or is it a very challenging vision, one that falls under the "in your wildest imagination" category?

Without an inspiring dream, life loses its zest, its purpose, its energy. As children leave the nest to start their own lives, many women—especially those who have chosen to remain home and raise their children—suffer from the "empty nest" syndrome. Their main purpose has been successfully fulfilled and now they must ask themselves what life is all about. Another common problem people face is becoming so busy helping others around them achieve their dreams that they forget to generate any dreams of their own. In addition, many men and women experience a midlife crisis as they reach or fail to reach certain goals, then suddenly realize that old age is fast approaching. They may either foolishly try to recreate their youth or reestablish new and meaningful dreams for the second half of their life.

I learned ten years ago when my life got too easy that without big dreams, I lost my energy and drive. I require challenges and wonderful, "impossible" dreams to energize my whole life process. Yet we are all different, and some people thrive on much more "do-able" dreams. Whatever your dreams, giving yourself permission to invest in them *is essential to high-energy living.*

Viktor Frankl, during his four-year imprisonment in a Nazi concentration camp, discovered that of the prisoners who escaped the gas chambers, those who had a life purpose (or dream) were far more likely to survive. Those who didn't, died. Bernie Siegel, a surgeon and teacher at Yale Medical School, and oncologist Carl Simonton also report that having a meaningful purpose is a primary factor for patients who successfully recover from cancer. In a new field of study called psychoneuroimmunology, we are learning that just thinking vividly about an exciting dream or goal, and imaging it as complete with all its benefits, can cause our body to create chemicals and hormones (such as endorphins) that balance our immune system, counter stress, and seem to create new energy.

Test this idea by recalling which people, in your experience, have the most dynamic energy. Do they have a dream and does it seem to energize them? Is their dream contagious to others around them? Martin Luther King's "I have a dream" speech is a wonderful example of this quality.

In addition, dreaming is a safe way to test options for the future. "If you can dream it, you can do it," said Walt Disney. I have a personal anecdote to share along this line. Several years ago in a workshop, I was encouraged to make a list of ten outrageous, inviting, challenging dreams for my life. If there were no limits, what would I wish? I made my list, but was careful to keep my ideas covered, for to me they were so impossible that I was embarrassed to have anyone else see them. Then a few years later I moved and was unpacking boxes. Out fell my list. At first I didn't recognize it. But as I read through the ten dreams, to my amazement, eight of the ten had been realized. I had earned my doctorate, published two books, started my own successful business, found and married a marvelous mate, designed and built a greenhouse, taken a year's sabbatical, enjoyed an exciting cruise in the Caribbean, and successfully designed the ideal career for myself.

We encourage you to entertain yourself each day with vivid images of your dreams as though they have come true in the best possible ways.

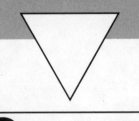

CHAPTER 3

ROLE MODELS FOR HIGH ENERGY:

Recapturing the Vitality of Childhood

66 *Great is the human who has not lost his childlike heart.* **99**
—Mencius (Meng-Tse), 4th century B.C.

66 *As usual, the serious me is working hard, but the real me is having fun.* **99**
—John Reed, CEO, Citicorp

66 *I'm still a small boy inside. I only got old on the outside.* **99**
—Stan L. Zundel, *I Climb to Live*

how many times have you watched your own children or the neighborhood kids and remarked enviously, "Where do they get all that energy?" or "They never seem to slow down!" or "Ah, to have that kind of energy again." Yes, childhood seems to be a time of limitless energy, the one period in our lives when we rarely felt tired, worn out, and pressed for time. Children seem to be in motion constantly—exploring, searching, risking, mimicking. But they also get a significant amount of rest during the day. And when their bodies tell them it's time to rest, they usually will switch gears to a more passive activity or will fall asleep wherever they are, then bounce into action again.

The Secret of Childhood Energy

Is there a way for us to maintain, or regain, much of the vitality we had in our youth? We believe there is. A supple body, hormonal growth spurts, and a high metabolism are not the only sources of children's vitality. Their behavior patterns and attitudes also contribute greatly to their energy levels. Consider the way healthy children go about their day, then compare this with the way you spend your average day. Study the list of fifteen childhood characteristics that we have observed among children.

Characteristics of Childhood

Little kids characteristically

1. seek out things that are fun to do, or else they find a way to have fun at what they are doing;
2. jump from one interest to another, leaving an activity whenever they feel bored or become more interested in something else;
3. are curious and usually eager to try anything once;
4. smile and laugh a lot;
5. experience and express emotions freely;
6. are creative and innovative;
7. are physically active;
8. are constantly growing mentally and physically;
9. will risk often—they aren't afraid to keep trying something that they aren't initially good at and aren't afraid to fail;
10. rest when their body tells them to (if they resist, they become cranky) and have shorter attention spans;
11. learn enthusiastically;
12. dream and imagine;
13. believe in the impossible;
14. generally don't worry or feel guilty; and
15. are passionate.

Unfortunately, most of us learned to "act our age" as we grew up. Yet this meant abandoning some of the most natural and powerful high-energy stimulants available to us. For example, remember how you felt the last time you were really angry at someone. Did you experience a surge of emotion and aggression flowing through your body, making it difficult to sit passively in your chair or the driver's seat? Did you feel like yelling at the offensive person, shaking your fists, or even striking the person? The incident might have left you so agitated that you had difficulty sleeping that night.

On a more positive note, what about the last time you achieved something wonderful? Perhaps you were chosen to receive a community award, or your ad campaign was selected over ten other companies vying for the commission, or you won your first game of tennis against a challenging partner. Can you remember the burst of emotion and momentum that surged through you? You probably wanted to shout for joy, jump up and down, and hug someone. And you probably were "revved up" for several days following the news.

What you experienced was a big dose of adrenaline or endorphins along with emotional energy coursing through your brain and body, making you alert and passionate and ready to respond. Of course, in most emotional situations, especially at the office, frequent unabashed displays of your feelings would be considered inappropriate and immature. So you probably had to do some deep breathing or aerobics to calm down those pent-up feelings, especially in the case of anger.

Or perhaps you have such "grown-up" control over your emotions that you can quickly talk yourself out of reacting to them. You regain your composure and keep the lid on. Often adults purposely never allow themselves to get too high or too low so that they can "retain their objectivity."

As adults and professionals we can't allow ourselves to be on an emotional roller coaster every hour of the day. Yet can  you recognize how this tempering of our feelings and actions stifles many of our most natural sources of energy? By eliminating most of our opportunities for fun, laughter, joy, physical activity, curiosity, adventure, and unrepressed emotional expression, we adults are in fact denying ourselves many positive energy boosts. Furthermore, we must expend a great deal of *mental* energy to repress *emotional*

ACTION ITEM

Examine your overall life-style and work day, and honestly ask yourself how many of the fifteen characteristics of childhood describe you now. Next think of the most active and successful adults you know and decide whether any of these traits fit their mode of behavior.

If you discover a large disparity between your current work/personality style and these characteristics of children, perhaps you have left behind some of the most valuable high-energy behavior traits of your youth. These normal childhood experiences and behavior patterns create a chemical change in our brain that releases new energy.

energy, as when we control our feelings of anger. Instead of leading the invigorating yet sufficiently restful life of a child, many of us have tied ourselves down to routine or to so many responsibilities that life becomes more exhausting than joyful. Is it any wonder we end up using artificial stimulants such as caffeine to perk us up and alcohol to loosen us up?

In addition to emotional expression, there is a strong link between play and energy. Normal children spend most of their day playing and having fun. Even when they are doing a chore for Mother and Dad, they often make a game out of it. And the fact that they are experiencing so much enjoyment and intrigue and so many adventures and emotional "highs" throughout the day is a major source of their high energy levels.

When adults "play with an idea" at work, they are also incorporating some of the elements of play. In addition, they let down mental barriers and relax the limits—or inhibitions—on their thinking. This allows for a greater flow of blood to the brain and for a release of energizing endorphins.

Being grown up doesn't have to mean leaving all our positive childhood traits behind. Victor H. Palmieri, who was brought in to help rehabilitate Mutual Benefit Life Insurance in New Jersey, said, "Strategies are okayed in boardrooms that even a child would say are bound to fail. The problem is, there is never a child in the boardroom!" We have experimented with a variety of ways to incorporate the fifteen energy-producing behavior patterns into the office and home environment. By relearning these strategies you can recapture much of the energy you had in your youth.

Our key discovery about high-energy adults was that their work and play styles were remarkably similar to those of children. And when we integrated these behavior styles into our own work habits and life-styles, our energy and productivity levels increased significantly as well.

Business Leaders Apply Traits of Childhood as Energy Builders

When we asked several corporate leaders which of the fifteen traits of childhood still fit them today, it was not unusual for their answer to be "*Most of them!*" Here are some comments from Peter Van Nort, president of ABB Nuclear Power, showing how he has retained these strategies:

1. **They seek out things that are fun to do, or else they find a way to have fun at what they are doing.** "I definitely seek out fun, and I find it difficult to push myself to do things that I don't view as fun. Of course, my definition of fun is different from a child's. Most of my activities at work are fun, even watering the plants in my office and cleaning off my whiteboard at the end of the day."

2. **They jump from one interest to another.** "I demand that I get to do that. I believe in responding to every mind stimulus unless it is truly hazardous. I feel free to pick up on my ideas as they come, to stop in midsentence if another thought hits me, and to jump from topic to topic."

3. **They are curious and usually eager to try anything once.** "I am always appalled when I sit through a meeting in which complex ideas and materials are being discussed, and many of the people aren't even taking notes. Yet they are supposed to understand this new information and bring it back to their staff. I know there is no way they

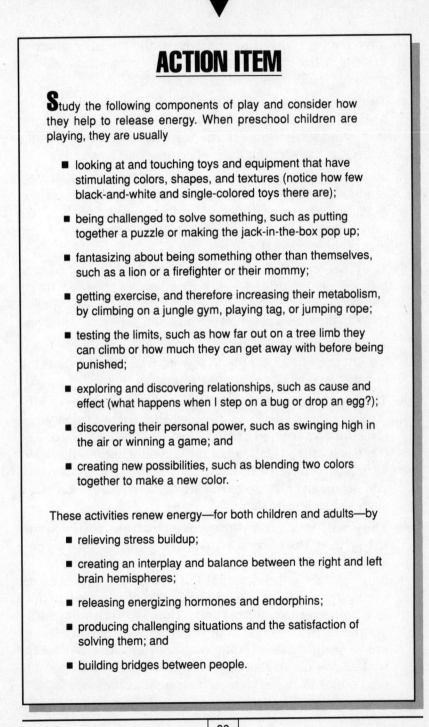

ACTION ITEM

Study the following components of play and consider how they help to release energy. When preschool children are playing, they are usually

- looking at and touching toys and equipment that have stimulating colors, shapes, and textures (notice how few black-and-white and single-colored toys there are);

- being challenged to solve something, such as putting together a puzzle or making the jack-in-the-box pop up;

- fantasizing about being something other than themselves, such as a lion or a firefighter or their mommy;

- getting exercise, and therefore increasing their metabolism, by climbing on a jungle gym, playing tag, or jumping rope;

- testing the limits, such as how far out on a tree limb they can climb or how much they can get away with before being punished;

- exploring and discovering relationships, such as cause and effect (what happens when I step on a bug or drop an egg?);

- discovering their personal power, such as swinging high in the air or winning a game; and

- creating new possibilities, such as blending two colors together to make a new color.

These activities renew energy—for both children and adults—by

- relieving stress buildup;

- creating an interplay and balance between the right and left brain hemispheres;

- releasing energizing hormones and endorphins;

- producing challenging situations and the satisfaction of solving them; and

- building bridges between people.

have really involved themselves in the learning process. Instead, I try to participate in every new situation that presents itself to me and to learn from it."

4. **They smile and laugh a lot.** "That's me. In fact, I refuse to have a picture taken when I'm not smiling. Sometimes a photographer will ask me for a serious, businesslike pose, but I never comply . . . because that's not me."

5. **They experience and express emotions freely.** "I definitely experience them freely. I only limit my expression of emotion to those times when the protocol of the situation will not allow it. Still, I'd say that I express my feelings 80 percent of the time."

6. **They are creative and innovative.** "This is simply the fine art of thinking of every problem as an opportunity and a challenge. The more I do this, the easier it gets. I truly believe this is what put me and others at the top!"

7. **They are physically active.** "I can feel the difference in my energy when I am physically active. This is a daily gift I give myself to boost my performance."

8. **They are constantly growing mentally and physically.** "I'm a strong believer in the idea that there are only two directions your mind can go—forward and backward. And there is no such thing as resting on your laurels. I don't feel very susceptible to the standard notions of age slowing you down, and I like to frequently learn new physical skills, such as juggling or skiing."

9. **They will risk often—they aren't afraid to try something that they aren't initially good at and aren't afraid to fail.** "In my line of work there is always a certain risk factor. I'd say that I'm not afraid to go against the system or to at least go back and challenge it. There is a tremendous opportunity that is often missed by people in business who never question the way things are . . . and what change might bring. Another factor that allows me to risk often is that I have absolute confidence that I will survive no matter what happens."

10. **They rest when their body tells them to.** "I try to respond

to my body's demands in many areas. If I feel tired and I'm in a situation where I can catch a nap, I'll do it."

11. **They learn enthusiastically.** "Definitely. For example, one thing I make a point to do when I fly is to sit next to someone interesting-looking and learn as much as I can about him or her."

12. **They dream and imagine.** "Absolutely. I can't imagine my life without my dreams."

13. **They believe in the impossible.** "I'll even go so far as to say that there is no such thing as the impossible. Now, I'm not saying that I want to try jumping out of a twenty-story window. But I believe that if you put your mind to something, you can find a way to do it. For example, recently my company was asked to overhaul and manufacture a particular piece of equipment. Some experts told us it would take at least sixty days, but we did it in thirty-seven. And with experience, now we have the time down to five and one-half days."

14. **They don't worry or feel guilty.** "I don't worry much and rarely dwell on guilt. I do spend time analyzing how I might have done something better. But once that's done, I feel I have resolved the matter. I basically feel satisfied if I know I have put my best effort into something, no matter how it turns out."

15. **They are passionate.** "That really leads back to feeling free to express my emotions and to being an avid learner. One of the fun things I have in my office is a baseball cap that says, 'I refuse to grow up.'"

Caution: It is important to remember that the traits of childhood we recommend must be combined with the judgment of adulthood. It is "childlike" rather than "childish" behavior that acts as an energy boost for adults. The big distinction between the two involves concern for other people. Childish behavior demands instant gratification no matter what inconvenience, upset, or problems it may cause for others. Childlike behavior encourages joy, creativity, and innovation while maintaining an equal concern for and sensitivity to the needs of others.

Energy Profiles

As you read the following excerpts from biographies and articles on Thomas Edison, Margaret Mead, Georgia O'Keeffe, Albert Schweitzer, Winston Churchill, and Liz Claiborne, notice how many of their behavior and work habits match the fifteen characteristics of children listed earlier.

Thomas Edison

Thomas Edison, the American father of invention, perfected the incandescent electric bulb, started the electrification of the United States, improved on the telephone and storage battery, made the first phonograph, and pioneered motion pictures—to name just a few of his accomplishments. In *Thomas Edison, American Inventor,* Roselyn and Ray Eldon Hiebert write, "From the time he was 12 years old until he reached his middle eighties he worked, often day and night. By trial and error he patiently attacked problems until he found their solutions."

Although Edison punched a time clock that recorded sixteen-hour days throughout his seventies, he also gave himself extended periods of leisure time away from work. He was fond of traveling and camping in the country with fellow inventors Harvey Firestone and Henry Ford and the naturalist John Burroughs. The Hieberts write: "Edison had a wonderful time on these trips. He loved to sit by the campfire at night and tell funny stories. He slept happily in his clothes, washed in the icy waters of mountain streams, and stopped to admire the views and vistas of the countryside." In addition, his "strict habits and demanding routine were balanced by a prankish sense of humor and zest for life."

This zest for life could be seen in his work nook as well. The Hieberts describe Edison's desk as being strewn with paperweights, bottles of chemical solutions, parts of phonographs, assorted incoming letters, a bottle of jelly, throat antiseptic, photographs, soda-mint tablets, and cubbyholes jammed with notes, reports, memoranda, and stale cigars. This very desk was an inspiration to another innovator. Henry Ford lovingly recreated Edison's lab and workplace in his

Greenfield Village, a museum of American life in the nineteenth century. Ford, the "father of mass production," who publicly scoffed at old methods, indulged his own enthusiasm and respect for past craftsmen and spent years and millions of dollars collecting and restoring old tools, machinery, artifacts, and buildings that reflected the creativity of the past.

Margaret Mead

Margaret Mead, America's foremost anthropologist, wrote thirty-four books and scores of articles, made ten films, lectured constantly across the United States and the world, frequently lobbied the government for more funding for scientific research, authored a monthly column for *Redbook* for some fifteen years, kept up with an extensive network of friends, and taught for many years at Columbia University. Writes Jane Howard in *Margaret Mead: A Life,* "With her daring journeys, provocative ideas and unbounded energy, she built on that celebrity [image] until she achieved the status of myth throughout the English-speaking world."

So remarkable were Mead's stamina and enthusiasm that one of her young colleagues mused on the need for a project "to study the source of her energy, her creativity, and her appetite for and ability to encompass the complexity of very many lives within her own life and intellect." Surely one source of her energy was her fervor to communicate her findings and to continuously gain new insights into a culture's effect on its people. Mead's passionate spirit was another wellspring of her energy. She invoked and evoked the best there was in other people.

Yet Mead enjoyed many hobbies and interests as well as her work, among them cooking, sewing, knitting, socializing, and raising her daughter, Mary Catherine Bateson. She believed in incorporating her child into her daily routine, as her parents had done with her. In every room of her house, reports Howard, were things for her daughter to play with. Beneath the coffee table was a shelf filled with sand so that Cathy could play while the grown-ups had cocktails. And next to Mead's dressing table was an easel so that Cathy could paint while her mother got dressed to go out.

"I expect to die, but I don't plan to retire," Mead said in her late sixties. Indeed, until she began to suffer from various illnesses in her last years, she seemed to attack her work with increasing vigor, calling it "post-menopausal zest." Leo Rosten commented that her insatiable curiosity kept her learning "all the time, through her pores. . . . She was the greatest picker of brains I've ever known, the greatest girl reporter in the world."

Of course, Mead needed to stop to "refuel" just like the rest of us. Like Edison, one way she restored her energy was to take catnaps whenever the opportunity presented itself. Once she passed up a formal prespeech luncheon in order to revive herself before giving her address. At other times she would instruct her staff to wake her up just minutes before she was to begin her speech.

Georgia O'Keeffe

Georgia O'Keeffe completed nearly 900 canvases depicting her unique vision of Southwest landscapes, clouds, flowers, stones, and evocative abstractions. She was always setting new goals and challenges for herself, using original hues of colors and trying difficult techniques. When her vision began to fail, she experimented with large sculptures and ceramics.

O'Keeffe usually painted intensely, from several hours up to an entire day if she was pleased with her results. But her work was often broken up by short, reviving breaks and "mini-vacations." Throughout her life, she balanced the stillness of her painting sessions with daily exercise.

O'Keeffe also had an emotional and joyful side. Her letters are riddled with exuberant feelings of love, astonishment, joy, uncertainty, and courage, all of which were manifested in her emotionally charged paintings.

Although she maintained many strong liaisons throughout her life, O'Keeffe also needed times of daily solitude. She took most of her walks alone, using the time to focus on the landscape and muse on the latest technique she was experimenting with. And although most of the male artists of her era made it plain to her that as a woman she couldn't hope to succeed, O'Keeffe stubbornly persevered. She continued producing her art until her death at age ninety-eight.

Albert Schweitzer

Nobel Prize–winner Albert Schweitzer was a physician, respected philosopher, renowned biblical scholar, prolific author, accomplished organist and organ builder, manager, and crusader for world peace. As committed as he was to his mission in Africa, he could not "surrender his gifts" of music, theology, writing, and lecturing, writes Robert Payne in *The Three Worlds of Albert Schweitzer*. Furthermore, Schweitzer shifted from project to project, interest to interest, throughout the day.

Despite Schweitzer's demanding schedule at the mission, he still needed recreation and a creative outlet. "Above all, his fruit orchard gave him intense pleasure," writes Payne, as did "the stimulus of music." Payne also notes that the doctor "worked better after playing seriously." Schweitzer once explained to someone who asked him the secret of his serenity, "Appreciate fantasy. When I play my piano in the evening in Lambaréné I shut my eyes and can make-believe I am playing a great organ and this gives me true repose."

Winston Churchill

Winston Churchill is best remembered as a brilliant statesman and military leader who had unflinching courage, fortitude, and energy. In fact, the British admiral J. H. Godfrey described Churchill as having "demonic energy and extraordinary imagination." A closer look at the man, through biographies and his own writing, reveals that much of his vitality and vision came from his ability to retain the sense of inventiveness, spontaneity, spunk, and belief in the impossible that children possess.

For example, in William Manchester's biography of Churchill, *The Last Lion,* Churchill is depicted as having a passionate "love of gadgetry and wildly improbable schemes." During the war, he was forever coming up with ideas for innovative types of weaponry, such as a trench-cutting tank. Although many of his inventive ideas seemed outlandish to his more conservative military leaders, he was not afraid to risk failure by trying what had never been conceived of before. This characteristic led Franklin Roosevelt to comment later, "Winston has fifty ideas a day, and three or four are good." Explains the author, "Most of his schemes were politely discussed and then dropped." But by the end of the war, many of Churchill's ideas were integrated into successful military strategy and weapons.

Churchill also had a fluid mind that "had many tracks, and if one was blocked, he left it and turned to another," writes Manchester. Furthermore, the prime minister had a strong artistic bent. He authored numerous biographies and history books, and in 1953 won the Nobel Prize for literature. In addition, he enjoyed painting and gardening in his retirement years.

Liz Claiborne

In 1976, already well into vibrant middle age, Liz Claiborne founded Liz Claiborne, Inc., a fashion enterprise that quickly grew into one of the youngest companies ever to land on the Fortune 500 list. She accomplished this feat as much through her ability to innovate, dream big, and risk often as through her sharp business sense. She captured a market that other designers had overlooked—the career woman over thirty who does not have the perfect figure of a fashion model and who prefers classic, softer styles and casual wear over short-lived trends.

Claiborne is often described as a "pathfinder" and a "reluctant revolutionary." Working for years as the chief designer for other clothing manufacturers, she tried unsuccessfully to convince her former bosses to create clothes for the older professional woman. Then, in 1976, she and her husband/partner risked their entire savings to market their own line of women's wear. The line was an immediate hit and quickly expanded into other areas including menswear, fragrance, and accessories. When Claiborne and her husband resigned from the board and sold their share of the company in 1990 to pursue other interests, they left an organization with almost no debt and $373 million in cash for stock buybacks, a dividend boost, and expansion—all from an initial investment of $255,000.

While building the company, Claiborne typically put in a ten-hour work day, but she knows the tricks for replenishing her energy supply. She often walked many blocks to work from her apartment and was a regular runner. In addition, she and her husband spent most weekends far removed from their work, walking, reading, and watching birds either at their beach house on Fire Island or their ranch in Montana. Claiborne does not seem to allow unrelieved stress, worries, or pent-up emotions to diminish her energy. People describe her as being intense but candid, witty, and fun-loving. Typical of high-energy people, Claiborne, well into her sixties, is preparing to pursue other dreams and ambitions now that her dream of a clothing line is a successful reality.

Retaining High-Energy Traits Throughout Adulthood

Charles Garfield in his book *Peak Performers, The New Heroes of American Business,* found that those who perform at high levels of energy and success followed the same patterns of behavior and thought as young children. Garfield's work reinforces the earlier, primary research done by Abraham Maslow. Maslow was the first psychologist who spent his career studying healthy as opposed to mentally ill people. He found that "self-actualized" people, who were able to achieve balance and outstanding performance and satisfaction in their lives, also followed the patterns we have described in our role models for high energy.

In addition to noticing how energetic and productive life can be for people in their sixties up to their nineties, we hope you saw many parallels between the behavior patterns of children and these men and women. We think these traits, plus a fervent dedication to their fields and a clear vision of what they wish to accomplish, are the primary reasons they were able to remain so highly energized. Outstanding leaders always seem to have a strong vision of where they are headed and what they are capable of doing, even when others consider that vision impossible. We remember as children setting out to build a fort. We would work tirelessly, dragging junk down the alley, hammering and building until after suppertime. Then we would beg to go back out after dark. There is enormous energy to be had from a goal if it is your personal dream. Yet only small children, fools, geniuses, and highly energetic people give themselves permission to dream so boldly.

The success of the energetic geniuses and business leaders profiled above also depended on several other traits that are not on our list for children. You probably can name them yourself. They are *perseverance, purpose,* and *discipline.* Unless someone is incredibly lucky, these traits usually make the difference between someone being highly successful or

just managing to get by. Actually, children know how to persevere or none of them would accomplish the arduous tasks of
learning to walk and talk. But since children appear to be having fun all the time, this quality isn't as obvious to us as we
watch them. Discipline, on the other hand, is a mature quality
that is acquired through practice and self-control.

Turning back to the high-energy behavior traits of children, how many similarities did you find between these traits
and the six adult profiles? Jot down some of your reactions in
the margins, if you wish.

First, did you notice that the adults profiled were avid
learners who were constantly experimenting with something
new? Edison was unwilling to rest on his past laurels but continued to improve on everything he invented. And O'Keeffe
went from black-and-white sketches to colored paintings to
sculptures in her later years.

Second, all of these highly successful men and women
were passionately involved in diverse interests and activities.
For example, Schweitzer could easily have become totally
consumed by his medical practice and mission, but he chose
not to deny himself the enjoyment and stimulation he received from the many other areas of his life.

Third, most of the people profiled worked on a variety of
projects during the day and would jump from one to the other
according to their moods and interests. Remember that this is
the normal play pattern of children, one that is often tagged
as a "short attention span." But this label would hardly be
used for geniuses who do three things at once.

Fourth, all the adults profiled were willing to try new
endeavors, to experiment and learn new skills, to become an
imperfect beginner at something. Churchill, Edison, and
O'Keeffe were so curious about some new aspect of their
work or plans that they were willing to start from scratch,
risking disappointment or even failure. Their highly developed sense of curiosity and adventure frequently led them
into new territories that challenged their creative and intellectual skills.

Fifth, most of these people believed in the value of play.
They broke away from their work to enjoy stimulating and

light-hearted activities by playing with their children, taking extended vacations, socializing with their co-workers and friends, decorating their offices with their favorite things (can't we call them toys as well?), and so on.

Finally, creativity and innovation were central to these people's work and activities, even among the nonartists.

If you are as convinced as we are that generating abundant and unlimited energy is linked to reclaiming many characteristics of childhood, you will want to test this hypothesis for yourself.

Learn to Let the Child Within You Live

Now let's look at some ways to help you tap into the abundant energy of kids. Four strategies that can be great fun will get you started. First, remember what it was that you loved doing as a child. Find ways to go back and indulge in these fond memories. Next ask what you missed out on that you longed to experience. Find ways to claim those adventures now. Then become aware of what inner fears and messages block or spoil your enjoyment. Creatively find ways to challenge or turn them off. And finally, you'll really get into the fun if you recruit an expert or two to coach you. Little kids are just such specialists, so be sure you let them take the lead, and notice the difference in how adults and little kids play.

We have collected a few high-energy stories from the research experiences of several of our participants to convince you to find your own ways to reclaim KidSpirit.

Tom Baker, executive vice president at TU Electric, shares his story:

"My daughter Kim graduated from Lake Highlands High School this spring (thank you, Lord!). At the end of each school year the senior class puts on a senior show in which they sing, dance, and perform skits. Three or four weeks before the show was to take place, I received a telephone call from another father. In a hushed voice he asked me to meet him along with several others at a local dance studio within the hour and not to say a word to Kim

ACTION ITEM

What was most fun for you when you were a child? Make a list of things you enjoyed. Invite a friend to join you as you remember together the good times of childhood.

Then add things you missed out on when you were a kid that would be joyful and energizing now. Think of all the things you wanted to do but didn't. Maybe you wanted to learn to play a musical instrument, paint, take photographs, or sail around the world. Dig up those old fantasies and start dreaming again. Here are some ideas to get you started:

- playing with paper dolls
- giving plays and shows
- digging a hole to China
- having water fights
- building a sailboat
- building soapbox racers
- making and flying kites

Let this list continue. Think of all the things you did—and those you wanted to do. Then begin to think of creative ways to enjoy your childhood pleasures and dreams. Claiming the joys of childhood can awaken that abundant energy resource in your life. Maybe you can become a Scout leader; in the process of helping youngsters discover new talents and fun, you might find some of your own. Perhaps you can enjoy that remote-controlled airplane that was beyond your budget when you were a kid.

When we validate our playful self by taking time to listen to and fulfill wishes and dreams, we bring back to life our optimistic, outrageous, enthusiastic, little-kid energy.

about it. He was asking fathers of graduating seniors to volunteer for a surprise skit in the school's senior show. I had no idea what to expect although I feared the worst. When I showed up at the appointed hour, I discovered that about thirty fathers were going to learn a dance routine, taught by one of the senior girls. We attended several secret practice sessions each week and learned a com-

plete routine to Michael Jackson's song 'Bad.' We dressed up in old jeans, Harley-Davidson T-shirts, and chains. I used about half a tube of Dep to slick my hair into a ducktail on the sides and combed the front forward into a point. Apply a couple of stick-on tattoos and there you have it. The act was appropriately called 'The Bad Dads' and, needless to say, it was the hit of the show.

It was interesting to watch a group of pinstriped captains of industry as we practiced and put on our skit. While we were getting dressed for one of the rehearsals, one of the Bad Dads commented that it was rather scary how comfortable some of us looked in our costumes! I actually had an increase in energy level after each rehearsal and experienced a bit of a 'high' after the performance. Recapturing the vitality of childhood works. I can't wait for my next trip back! That trip will be in a few weeks when I put the pinstripe back in the closet and get out the Harley T-shirt when the family vacations in Walt Disney World. I can't wait to ride the rides!!"

Each of us has dreams we missed out on while growing up. These can be even more delicious to realize as an adult, after waiting decades to claim them. For me such a dream was to learn to tap dance.

As a girl we couldn't afford the shoes or the lessons. So at the age of forty-nine I bought a pair of shiny black tap shoes and a videotape called "Let's Tap" by Bonnie Franklin and learned three dances to perform for my fiftieth birthday! This generated lots of new energy for me, and it was a great way to enjoy aerobic exercise. To my amazement, many of my friends who had learned to tap dance as kids were also excited when I invited them to tap again as adults in a playful birthday-party recital.

John Shawn Tawgin chalked up sales of $7 million in 1990 by having fun and watching others have fun. He began his career in advertising and soon found that the job wasn't satisfying. He moved on to photography, a hobby he enjoyed, but again found that he spent a lot of time trying to create an illusion of fun for photos. Finally, he decided to find people who actually were having a good time. He began taking pictures of people at amusement parks—flying down the roller coaster, swooping around the Ferris wheel, splashing through a waterfall. Today John Shawn Productions takes pictures at fifteen amusement parks and has fifty full-time and 600 part-time employees. And John is having a good time, too.

I must have built ten or twelve tree houses in my early days, never as grand as those I could build now. This past year I gave myself permission to build a marvelous tree house as a second-floor addition to our home, which surrounds a favorite sweet gum tree in our backyard. It has a dumbwaiter that lifts things up into the tree house. A group of engineers built a wonderful tire swing that hangs invitingly from a nearby live oak. A shiny red spiral stairway allows adults easy access to the tree house. And I am amazed at how much energy we get by giving ourselves permission to live this fantasy.

At age sixty-seven, the great author Leo Tolstoy enjoyed his first bicycle lesson and spoke of it as rewarding him with

"a sense of boyish pleasure." It is equally interesting to note that his forty-one-year-old secretary disapproved, feeling that "such a frivolous pursuit was not consistent with Tolstoy's current position as a world leader of morality." One of our biggest energy robbers is the blocking assumption that child-like fun is inappropriate for responsible adults, when in fact, keeping our lives filled with joyful purpose may be our most significant way to preserve health, sanity, and balance.

We have encouraged the executives in our Perspective III program (executive development seminars that teach the benefits of whole-brain thinking) to spend time with very young children to learn how they play and how they process or think as they play. The idea was to see what we can learn from them and how we might use these insights to develop our right-brain thinking.

Bob Gary, a Dallas executive, tells this story, which illustrates the fresh perspective children bring to our lives.

"The Lord must have realized that folks need a shot in the arm when they get to my age because He gave us grandchildren. They are great examples of high energy, always ready for hugs, always giving out great, long belly laughs. Yet as adults, we are taught not to behave this way even though physical affection gives us a great emotional boost.

Kids instinctively know how to have high energy. Just watch them breathe deeply all the time. And everything they do, they give their all through their laughter, play, and emotions.

Another lesson we can learn from kids is that they seem to know how to avoid things that will steal their energy. Back when my grandson was three years old, he had the irritating habit of saying 'I don't like you.' It was driving everyone up the wall. One day I had him on the tractor with me and he said it again. So I asked him what he would do if I told him that I didn't like him. 'I wouldn't listen to you,' he answered. What he meant was that he wouldn't give someone else permission to hurt him. If you let someone hurt you—and others can't really hurt you

ACTION ITEM

What stops you from awakening childhood energy? Make a list of "funstoppers" (admonishments from others or yourself that discourage participation in childhood activities). Some examples are:

"What will the neighbors think?"

"Don't start anything you're not going to finish!"

"Grow up!"

"Be perfect!"

"Anything worth doing is worth doing well!"

"You look ridiculous. Don't make a fool of yourself."

"What will my friends think?"

Be sure you don't contaminate your energy-building fun with adult expectations. If you hear these kinds of warnings creeping into your consciousness, it might help to stop and acknowledge their potential effect on you by writing them in the margin. Then realize that they come from an entity we call the Merciless Taskmaster. It's the part of you that expects you to adhere to the all-work-and-no-play Puritan ethic, that won't accept any tasks done less than perfectly and completely, that cares more about other people's expectations of you than your own needs. Turn off that nagging taskmaster voice long enough to discover how much fun and energy you can get by unleashing your natural instincts for free, creative play and hobbies.

Where can you find an energy coach to relearn the secrets of getting energy from your fun? Find a child to play with! If you find it difficult to turn off adult "should" messages, a child can be a good role model. Being with children often gives us permission to open and explore our playful right brain without contaminating the wonder and fun with left-brained restrictions. Collect a list of possible playmates who could become your energy coaches—perhaps a kid down the block or a grandchild.

unless you allow them to—then you're also letting pent-up hurt drain your energy from you. Of course the flip side to that is that nobody will love you without your permission, either. So if you want to build up your energy, let someone express kindness and love to you."

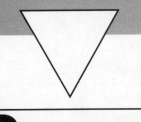

BALANCING WORK AND PLAY:

Are You Joy-Starved?

66 *Over the years, I've had many executives come to me and say with pride: 'Boy, last year I worked so hard that I didn't take any vacation.' It's actually nothing to be proud of. I always feel like responding, 'You dummy. You mean to tell me that you can take responsibility for an $80 million project and you can't plan two weeks out of the year to go off with your family and have some fun?* **99**

—Lee Iacocca, *Iacocca: An Autobiography*

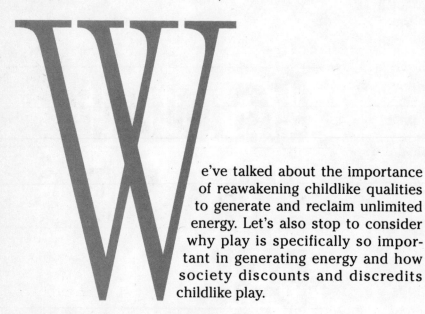

e've talked about the importance of reawakening childlike qualities to generate and reclaim unlimited energy. Let's also stop to consider why play is specifically so important in generating energy and how society discounts and discredits childlike play.

The All-Work, No-Play Mentality

It is easy to fall into an all-work, no-play mentality in our culture. As author and social critic Jeremy Rifkin writes in his book *Time Wars,* "The modern age has been characterized by a Promethean spirit, a restless energy that preys on speed records and shortcuts . . . existing only for the quick fix. . . . Despite our alleged efficiency . . . we seem to have less time for ourselves and far less time for each other. . . . We have become more organized but less spontaneous, less joyful."

Many businesses, including private law practices, public relations and advertising firms, large corporations, and owner-operated companies, consider a work week of sixty to ninety hours as routine. In addition, the United States has one of the shortest average vacation leaves in the industrialized world. In most Western European nations, a five-week vacation leave is standard for new as well as longtime employees.

Maternity and paternity leaves are also much more generous for our European counterparts.

The U.S. business world's mentality tends to be: the more hours worked, the more work produced. This idea applies not only to the stretch of hours worked on a given day and week but also to the minimal amount of personal break time allotted to each day. Yet for many reasons, this myth of a productivity curve continually rising throughout the day is being refuted. Numerous studies show that people usually hit a productivity peak at a certain point each day (or over a span of a certain number of hours worked); then their efficiency, carefulness, motivation, and creativity steadily wane. Working much beyond that effective productivity point, when fatigue is setting in, will often result in errors, poor judgment, accidents and injuries, and overall uninspired thinking. In the area of learning, other studies indicate that sixty-minute periods may be the maximum time a person can comprehend and process information at his or her peak learning level. Steadily decreasing mental and physical energy levels are the primary causes of decline in each of these areas.

There is a way, however, to stay alert and productive throughout an average work day. Our method involves restoring your energy reserves *before* they have dropped too low. Our studies clearly support the value of *integrating a variety of short, brain-balancing energy breaks into each work day*.

A growing number of businesses are incorporating these energy-renewing breaks into their work structure and environment. For instance, at E. I. Du Pont de Nemours and Company, employees have scheduled frequent breaks to juggle, walk, do puzzles, and draw maps in the company's recreation room. At a huge shipping firm in Sweden, the staff often relax and test their new ideas in "the Brain Room," a converted storage area that features employee artwork, classical music, comfortable chairs, and brainstorming tools like flip charts and colored pens.

Within our own company in Dallas, we encourage our team to balance intensive, demanding work periods with frequent energy breaks. Most of us are on flextime, which means we are accountable to get our part of the job done but can plan around our personal and family needs. Rayo, our production director, takes an extended lunch break every other day to play basketball at a nearby YMCA and chooses to work later in the evenings. Our office is closed from noon to 1:00 P.M. to ensure time for an energy-restoring lunch break. Often two or three of us will take a brisk twenty-minute walk when we need an energy lift. There are also musical instruments for music breaks. A stationary bike invites anyone to take an exercise break. Some days there are morning breaks for peppermint tea and muffins and afternoon fruit and cheese breaks outside on the deck. Errands might include a joy break to stop by a toy store or card shop and browse for new ideas for our seminars. There are frequent five-minute breaks to celebrate news of a client's creative breakthrough or personal growth.

In addition, we each have a learning partner within the team. We become role models for each other as we review our creative plans for work *and* play. We share stress management strategies and make a serious personal commitment to live what we teach and then teach each other from our experience. Each of us also invites our family and friends to participate and teach us from their experiences. This process brings abundant energy into our team.

The Link Between Play and Energy

Play and leisure time are critical and essential to maintaining abundant energy because they

1. allow the left hemisphere to rest while the right hemisphere creates new options and possible solutions to problems;

2. help release built-up tension;

3. can open blocked thinking and trigger creative ideas;

4. stimulate an energy boost and thus restore your energy resources;

5. build bridges between people;

6. create hormones, endorphins, and other neuropeptides that balance your immune system;

7. allow you to safely explore new perspectives and new interests; and

8. create new links between ideas.

Often, as we become adults, we lose our capacity to play. We may participate in games or sports, but we do so with our serious, ego-centered, competitive, "do your best" left brain hemisphere. In order to accomplish the goal of energy renewal and refreshment, we simply need to learn to shift gears and participate from the right hemisphere of our brain, which is open, spontaneous, flexible, joyful, loving, and eager to play for no purpose other than to enjoy experiencing and possibly sharing the moment.

If you find yourself on the golf course or tennis court working hard to do it right, irritated because you are playing badly, or feeling tense about doing your best, then try to relax, be gentle with yourself, and remind yourself that you need to shift gears. To get the full benefit from play, first you need to learn to love yourself unconditionally just because you are you rather than because you are good at something. Next, extend that love to others and to life itself. Then just enjoy being and sharing and laughing and being open to all that is. Can you remember this wonderful open quality of childhood, demanding nothing from self or life other than to simply participate in life? Learning to play is a critical step in discovering abundant energy.

The Link Between Play and Well-Being

As Norman Cousins reported in *Anatomy of an Illness,* joyful laughter causes the brain to create endorphins that relieve stress and open and balance the immune system. These neuropeptides also seem to be linked to energy renewal. Notice the next time you leave a high-pressured meeting and have a few minutes of joyful laughter and relaxed, playful talk with a trusted friend. You are very likely to feel a sense of renewal, find new balance to your judgment, and make a fresh commitment to appropriate priorities. The same is true of any type of play that stimulates the senses, such as listening to music, seeing colorful photos and drawings, or drinking a delicious glass of juice.

Just as happy thoughts create endorphins, stressful situations can also change brain chemistry. When we are tired, trying hard, overcommitted, and possibly overwhelmed by the unending demands on our time, our brains get flooded with adrenaline and other chemicals that result from crisis messages. Our bodies work this way to protect themselves from physical harm. When we are (or think we are) in danger, the blood rushes away from the brain and digestive process into the extremities and becomes thicker so it can coagulate faster. This is all good if in fact we are about to be gnawed by a bear, but the results also include labored heartbeat, higher blood pressure, shallow breathing, less oxygen to the brain, and slowed-down thinking ability. You can see that this physical situation is counterproductive to making good decisions and thinking creatively.

Understanding the chemistry of the brain helps us learn how to deal with problems more effectively. We realize that competing relentlessly, trying harder even when we're exhausted, or trying to win by intimidation not only don't work; they are positively counterproductive. For our best effort, we need the chemicals that come from feeling safe, challenged, supported, and excited about the possibilities of making a difference. Notice that we aren't suggesting either a purely safe, enjoyable environment or a scary, intimidating situation. Having some of both the elements of risk (challenge) and fun (trust) makes the difference. The risk/challenge part gives us the sense of urgency and energy needed. The fun and trust give us room to think differently and discover or create a better way to do more with less.

The paradox of opposites is typically present. That's what this book is about. By learning to draw on the opposites of the two sides of the brain, by learning to think of problems as opportunities, by learning to trust and team with others who are not like us, we can gain and learn an infinite amount. Synergy is the result of teaming with opposites. And, by definition, synergy takes place when the whole is worth more than the sum of the parts.

The Link Between Play and Innovation

Stop for a moment and recall the times of your best ideas, your breakthrough solutions. Maybe you came up with a way to resolve a staff dispute, to phrase a perfect slogan for your new ad campaign, or to end a short story you were writing. Try to recall where you were and what you were doing when the creative "Aha!" popped into your head.

If your experiences have been similar to those of the many inventors and artists we have studied, you probably got that wonderful idea not when you were struggling to find an answer, but precisely when you weren't trying to think about it. Perhaps you were on the running path, in the shower, at a symphony concert, reading the funnies, or driving home from work. For many people, their great "Aha!" moments of insight come when they wake up in the middle of the night.

Psychologist Rollo May, in *The Courage to Create,* discusses "the necessity of alternating work and relaxation, with the insight often coming at the moment of the break between the two, or at least within the break." Likewise, he details a personal breakthrough that came to him after he had spent an exhausting day struggling with a conflicting set of data. "I was tired. I tried to put the whole troublesome business out of my mind. About 50 feet away from the entrance to the Eighth Street station, [the answer] suddenly struck me 'out of the blue.'"

Quoting from the autobiography of the brilliant mathematician Jules-Henri Poincaré, May cites a fascinating pattern to these moments of insight. Poincaré wrote that for fifteen days he strove to prove a theory but "reached no results." Then, he reports: "One evening, contrary to my custom, I drank black coffee and could not sleep. Ideas rose in crowds; I felt them collide until pairs interlocked, so to speak, making a stable combination. By the next morning I had established the existence of a class of Fuchsian functions, those which come from the hypergeometric series; I had only to write out the results, which took but a few hours." After a frustrating struggle, suddenly everything became crystal clear to him. Poincaré documented many such breakthrough ideas coming while he was relaxing, physically removed from his work.

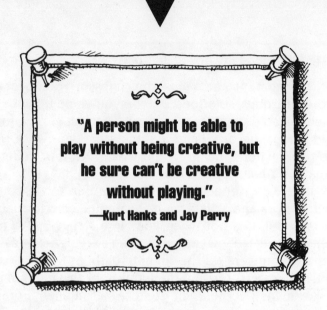

"A person might be able to play without being creative, but he sure can't be creative without playing."
—Kurt Hanks and Jay Parry

One reason the brain needs to be distracted from the problem it is being asked to solve is that it can get deadlocked. When forced to concentrate too long on the same problem, the brain can end up going in circles, rehashing the same factors, coming to the same end point again and again. In the future when you think you've come to a stalemate, put the problem aside, take a relaxing break, and turn to some other work for a while (or until the next day if possible). If you've been working with no progress for an entire week, try to totally block the problem and related pressures from your mind for several days. Then, as your conscious mind is allowed to switch hemispheres and focus on other topics, the subconscious mind can take over the details of the problem you need to solve. Many theorists say that the subconscious mind has greater access to the huge storehouse of data in your brain and that it operates much more freely when you are sleeping or are engaged in an entertaining, or "mindless," activity. The subconscious can also break through to the surface of your conscious mind more easily while you are in a relaxed, nonworking state.

A word of caution is due, however, before we go on. If you begin to *expect* your play to produce creative thoughts, this will destroy the relaxed, free-thinking nature of your play. So learn to play strictly to enjoy yourself and to revive your energy.

Child-Like Versus Child-Ish

Many adults, when they first try to go back and rediscover the secrets of childhood energy, do so in a childish way. Think about the major difference in these approaches. What comes to mind?

When we are childish, we are focusing on our own needs and wishes with little or no awareness or concern for others. It is childish behavior to refuse to turn down your radio while your officemate is trying to concentrate on a difficult report.

When we are childlike, on the other hand, we enjoy the benefits of both adult and child responses. You can benefit from joy and fun *without losing sight of the complex good judgment of adulthood.* Childlike fun is never at the expense of other people or objectives. When you are childlike, you retain all the benefits of your adult wisdom and concern for others while rejuvenating yourself with the freedom, joy, abandon, and passion of the child. Here is where synergy kicks in. When you use both the adult and the child fully, you gain an enormous, illogical benefit. One plus one equals seven—or more!

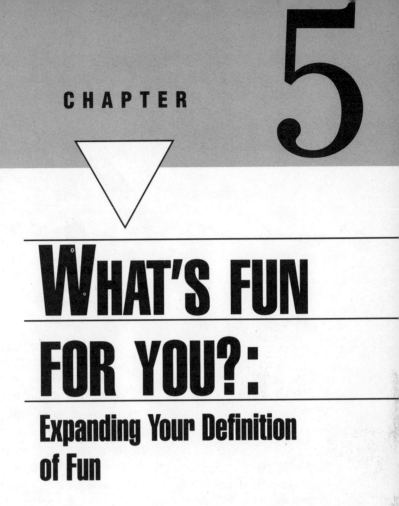

WHAT'S FUN FOR YOU?:

Expanding Your Definition of Fun

66 *There's no reason that work has to be suffused with seriousness. . . . Professionalism can be worn lightly. Fun is a stimulant to people. They enjoy their work more and work more productively.* 99

—Herb Kelleher, CEO, Southwest Airlines

66 *When you are completely absorbed or caught up in something, you become oblivious to things around you, or to the passage of time. It is this absorption in what you are doing that frees your unconscious and releases your creative imagination.* 99

—Dr. Rollo May

ne of the basic prob-
lems for most adults is
twofold: not only do they
have trouble finding time to
play, but when it comes right
down to it, they have lost touch
with what's fun for them. The
Action Item in this chapter will help
you test your Fun Quotient. Before reading on, it is important
to complete the inventory in the Action Item so that you will
get an unbiased insight into your current awareness level.

When I first tried the inventory, most of my ideas appeared
on the second half of the sheet and were such lengthy under-
takings that I was not likely to ever get around to them. One
activity was making a wall hanging of stitchery to cover one
wall of the bedroom. I envisioned converting a bedroom into a
sewing room and working about a year on the project. Another
idea was to buy a potter's wheel and make hand-built pottery.
This would require converting a room into a studio, building a
damp room for drying the clay, putting in a special commercial
drain, and spending about $2,000 on special equipment.

Then I began to realize that perhaps I didn't have inner
permission to have fun. If I really wanted to make hand-built
pottery, all I had to do was to enroll in an art course at the
community college, which was about ten minutes from my
home. In less than a week and with about $40 in tuition,
I would be enjoying this process.

ACTION ITEM

Jot down things that are fun for you. Put them into columns according to the amount of time they take: 2–5 Minutes, 5–30 Minutes, 30 Minutes to 1/2 Day, and 1/2 Day or More. As you begin recalling what's fun for you, write down as many possibilities as you can. For example, you might think, "It's fun to read a novel." How long do you typically need to enjoy this fun? "Well, I'd like to have at least an hour to get into it," you might answer. So you would enter this idea for fun in the third column, "30 Minutes to 1/2 Day." An idea for fun might fit in all four columns, such as spending time with a special friend. Time how long it takes before you begin to run out of ideas. Draw a line when you find the ideas are no longer coming quickly and you have to stop and think awhile between ideas.

Take time for this list-making activity. If you like, invite a friend or mate to make a similar fun list while you make yours.

How many activities did you come up with? You might be interested to know that most busy adults run out of ideas after they've thought of ten to fifteen. (Ten-year-olds have easily generated fifty-five ideas in the same amount of time.) How many could you think of quickly before having to really search for ideas?

Count up how many ideas you have in the first two columns (ways to have fun in thirty minutes or less) and how many you have in the last two columns. Which has the larger number? What does this tell you about the problems you are having finding time for fun?

2–5 Minutes	5–30 Minutes	30 Minutes to 1/2 Day	1/2 Day or More

As I analyzed my fun inventory I discovered that I knew of very few ways to have fun that required less than thirty minutes. *Yet most of my free time came in small bits.* I also realized that because I didn't have permission to have fun, I kept it safely out of reach by dreaming up projects so lengthy or expensive that I couldn't find the time or money to get into them.

The third way I was missing out on fun was by not planning ahead so that I had the supplies I needed when I had a few free minutes between projects or phone calls. If you come to work armed with ideas for short breaks and any accessories you'll need (such as fishing, golf, or special-interest magazines, a portable tape player with earplugs and your favorite relaxing music, colored pens and drawing paper, a puzzle, or a book of your favorite cartoons), you can easily find time to schedule some moments of fun and relaxation into each work day. And you will achieve a healthy balance of work and refreshing play or relaxation time during the week instead of postponing fun for the weekend.

With these three insights, I began to reorganize my work/play quotient. I made the longest list I could of ways to have fun in two to five minutes, and I would urge you to do the same. We have included some of our ideas to get you started. Don't stop till you get at least twenty or thirty good ideas.

Two- to Five-Minute Breaks

1. Read the comics or your favorite columnist in the paper.
2. Listen to a favorite song with a tape recorder and headphones.
3. Close your eyes and visualize yourself skiing down a slope.
4. Plan something enjoyable for that evening or weekend.
5. Lay your head on the desk for a five-minute nap.
6. Check the movie schedule in the daily paper.
7. Call a friend and plan a lunch date.
8. Praise a secretary or co-worker for a job well done.
9. Browse through a catalog or art book.
10. Look at travel brochures and plan your next vacation.
11. Play with a toy you keep at the office, such as a yo-yo, kaleidoscope, paddle ball, or dart board.

12. Take a walk around the block or around the office.
13. Work on a crossword puzzle.
14. Tell someone a joke.
15. Breathe deeply or meditate for five minutes.
16. Wash your face.

Then go to your daily schedule and begin to plan your play as thoughtfully and creatively as you do your work. For the first week, you might just practice taking several two- to five-minute joy breaks each day. Observe both the quality of your energy and the quality of your work and mental processing right after your joy breaks. We think you will find a noticeable improvement in all three areas. On the way home each day, mentally reward yourself for using this new process.

Five- to Thirty-Minute Breaks

Now you are ready to make a longer list of ways to have fun in five to thirty minutes. Again, you'll enjoy this more and will get a much better list if you do it with a friend or two. We have included some of our favorite ideas to prime the pump.

1. Listen to some inspiring or career development ideas from a seminar cassette tape.
2. Learn French or another language on cassette.
3. Plan extra walking into your day—park a brisk walk away from your office or the grocery store.
4. Read an article in a favorite magazine.
5. Select and order a present for a friend or yourself from a favorite mail order catalog.
6. Take a sack lunch and a good book to a nearby park.
7. Stop by a bookstore to browse.
8. Have a collection of activities, hobbies, and crafts that you can easily pick up and put down, such as whittling, needlework, weaving, puzzles, single-hand card games, juggling, and crossword puzzles.
9. Carpool with someone you enjoy. Try to focus your conversation primarily on positive, energy-building topics.
10. Plan something special to look forward to this evening, making whatever arrangements are necessary.

11. Plan a surprise for someone you love or appreciate, such as a phone call or a note placed in a coat pocket.
12. On your way to work, have breakfast with someone you enjoy.
13. Take a different route home from work, stopping to walk in a beautiful neighborhood, to sit by a pond, to shop at a rural produce stand, or simply to drive through the countryside with your windows down.

Weekday evenings require special planning because typically there are several routine chores to fit into that time and not a lot of open time just for fun. Also, if you wait until evening to decide upon and arrange your break, you may be too tired to even consider what would be enjoyable that evening. Thus, we recommend making a habit out of choosing at least one thing to look forward to each evening, even if it's only twenty minutes for a neck massage or fast gin game. In addition, planning ahead so that you anticipate your evening fun will give you another, earlier energy boost.

Weekday Evenings: Fun Ideas in Thirty Minutes to Two Hours

To whet your appetite, consider the following list of after-work activities that can be done in thirty minutes to two hours.

1. Enjoy making music on the piano, guitar, kazoo, or whatever you play. Learn to have fun playing badly. Most of us learned to play some instrument as kids but gave it up because we didn't enjoy lessons. Play just for the fun of it this time. Put together trios and quartets of strange combinations as you renew early interests in the piano, clarinet, trombone, or drums.
2. Take a long walk and watch the sunset.
3. Trade rubs for sore feet, backs, or necks with your family.
4. Have a cookie-baking evening and make several kinds to freeze for later. Mail them to kids in college or take them to work to share with the office team.
5. Get out old games—checkers, dominoes, Parcheesi,

Monopoly, or puzzles—and have an ongoing tournament for the week. The winner takes the loser to dinner and a movie, or prepares dinner for the loser. Short games make good homework breaks for students.

6. Call or write someone special you've been out of touch with; tracking down lost friends can be half the fun. Most people will be flattered by your interest.

7. Break out of your routine. For example, enjoy a chilled cup of fresh juice or gazpacho before preparing dinner while sharing pleasant thoughts from your day.

8. Plan your next vacation—collect maps, books, articles, or vacation lore from friends. Center a trip around a special interest (opera, Indian ruins, botany). Planning a trip well in advance not only saves you money and headaches but also allows for more options and spontaneous fun once you're on your way. And planning, like reminiscing afterward, stretches your enjoyment of your vacation over time.

9. Join the family in a game of backyard badminton, croquet, Ping-Pong, or hide-and-seek before dinner.

10. Review old pictures with your parents and tape their memories to accompany them. What treasures for later years and generations!

11. While the weather is good and sunsets are late, enjoy gardening. Trade cuttings from favorite plants with a neighbor; create designs on sand or pebble surfaces that you can change with your moods or the seasons (an idea taken from Japanese gardening).

12. Get out old musical albums and enjoy memories of years gone by. Dance in your own living room.

13. Spend an evening making a long list of things that would be fun to do, people it would be fun to see, places you've always wanted to visit.

14. Keep a journal—pick a format you really enjoy so it's not a chore. You can even keep a journal of delightful developments and quotes from a growing child. Looking back at old journal entries can provide perspective, surprises, insights, direction, and energy.

15. Have a bad day? Role play with your friends and/or family about outrageous, silly things you might have done dif-

ferently or might have said to people who tried your patience. (Laughter is a great cure for relieving pent-up stress and frustration.)

Half-Day or Longer Breaks: A Mini-Vacation a Week

Just as weekdays are focused on achieving work goals, to maintain a balance between work and play, weekends need to be focused on renewal. So even if you are a single parent or both you and your spouse work outside the home, be sure to look forward to some part of each weekend, even if it's only an hour or two. We credit Tim Hansel with his wonderful idea of planning for fifty-two mini-vacations a year. In his book *When I Relax I Feel Guilty,* he helps readers rediscover the vital role of recreation in their lives. Doesn't the idea of having a vacation waiting for you at the end of every week sound great?

You can have lots of fun just generating your list (unless you feel trapped by your schedule or circumstances and are unable to claim even the most meager play time). Use brainstorming. At first many of the ideas do seem unlikely. But as the list grows, so does our awareness of ways we can fit more and more enjoyment into our lives.

We present here ideas for half the year. See if you can supply ideas for the other half. Each part of the country has its own special sites, festivals, and opportunities, so let our list remind you of opportunities in your area.

1. Ride in a hot-air balloon or go to a balloon festival.
2. Visit a zoo or a museum.
3. Locate an environmental center in your area and take a class such as natural basketry. Bring home wildflower seeds for your own yard.
4. Have a stay-home-and-sleep-in vacation, complete with breakfast in bed.
5. Get off the beaten path and take a ride through the country or interesting but out-of-the-way parts of the city.
6. Check out the farmers' markets in your area. They provide fresh fruits, vegetables, nuts, and local flavor and can be a great place to talk with interesting people.

7. Attend a music festival. Plan your own. Provide nonmusicians with spoons, tambourines, or perhaps a string bass made of a washtub, broomstick, and tight string.
8. Plan a bicycle trip.
9. Go horseback riding.
10. Enjoy a massage from a professional masseuse.
11. Recall some of the playful things you did as a kid. Teach them to others or to your own kids.
12. Go square dancing or folk dancing, or sign up to learn push dancing or other styles you may not know.
13. Go on a wildflower-picking or photography hike.
14. Pack a lunch and enjoy a picnic. There are lots of unusual kites to build and fly. Or if the weather turns bad, spread out your blanket at home and be glad there are no ants!
15. Take some fun and love to the elderly and celebrate life and living together.
16. Go rock climbing. Learn new skills from an expert.
17. Go roller skating or ice skating. Take lessons if this is new for you.
18. Change roles for a fresh outlook on life. Whoever usually cooks, drives, selects the entertainment, or cleans the kitchen swaps roles with a partner. There can be a bonus of renewed appreciation for each other.
19. Visit a state fair. Plan to enter next year.
20. Take a let's-learn-something-new vacation. Visit the library or bookstore for ideas to get you started.
21. Have a spiritual growth weekend. Retreat to the woods with reading material to challenge or expand your spiritual awareness. Plan time to be alone and listen.
22. Go to a garage sale, estate sale, or auction.
23. Find a hotel with special mini-vacation rates. You don't even have to leave town for a get-away treat.
24. Go bowling or play miniature golf.
25. Throw a "heroes' party." Invite your friends to come dressed as their favorite hero.
26. Rent a Winnebago or camper for a weekend getaway.

" *When my work pile is getting deeper than I can handle or want to handle, I'll let myself get lost in my picture of West Texas bluebonnets on the wall.* **"**

—C. R. Oliver, President, Hydrocarbon Sector, Fluor Daniel, Inc.

JUGGLING, JOGGING, AND JOKING:

Slotting Energy Breaks into Your Work Day

❝ *I feel sorry for people who don't enjoy their jobs. I can't imagine what it would be like to wake up in the morning and not look forward to work. Now, before I schedule vacation, I check to see what I will be missing at work. I will never miss another Halloween!* **❞**

—**Tonda Montague, Manager,**
Employee Communications,
Southwest Airlines

ow that you have considered an
array of ways to have fun as an
adult—especially fun that can
be grabbed in short five- to
sixty-minute increments—you
are ready to start incorporating
these fun breaks into your work day. And by experimenting
with the ideas and suggestions in this chapter, we hope that
you quickly feel the high-energy boost that comes from
achieving a better balance between work and play.

Four Energizing Daily Maintenance Times

First, focus on four times during the working day when most
people either lose energy or overlook the possibility of putting
fresh energy into their day: getting ready for work, commuting
to work, eating lunch, and commuting from work. Most people
devote from two and one-half to four hours per day to these
activities. Think about how you use these four periods.

Do you review the day as you are getting ready for work
in the mornings, worried about what might go wrong, what
you might forget or not get to, or how far behind you are
already? (Is this an energy drain?) Do you lose any energy listening to the news? Driving to work, what do you think about?
Do you allow traffic to drain your energy? Do you rehearse
what you will say to this person or that person? Is it positive
or negative? Are you gaining or losing energy?

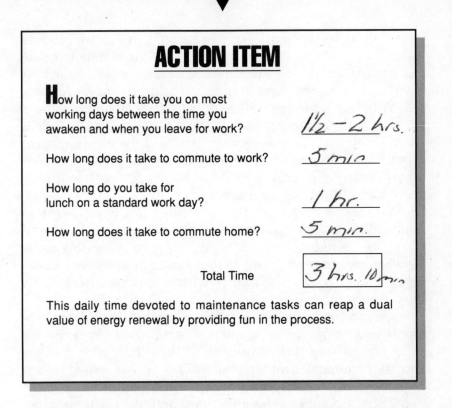

ACTION ITEM

How long does it take you on most
working days between the time you
awaken and when you leave for work?   *1½ – 2 hrs.*

How long does it take to commute to work?   *5 min*

How long do you take for
lunch on a standard work day?   *1 hr.*

How long does it take to commute home?   *5 min.*

Total Time   *3 hrs. 10 min*

This daily time devoted to maintenance tasks can reap a dual
value of energy renewal by providing fun in the process.

Later, over lunch, how do you spend your time? Do you
ever plan a wonderful lunch with a special friend, then make the
mistake of contaminating the time by focusing on problems? Do
you often eat lunch in your office while continuing to work? Or
do you grab a fast-food lunch on the run while doing errands for
your household and family? And does the food you choose
leave you feeling energized or sluggish an hour later?

The point to these questions is to see how much of this
time you consciously spend putting energy back into your
own system. Realize that if you do this, your energy boost will
be contagious—your lunch partner or work associate will feel
it, too.

Now think of how you spend the time during the commute home in the evening. It is not unusual to focus on what
you did wrong that day, what work you failed to get to, or how
much work is still stacked up on your desk, waiting for you.
Note that all three of these thoughts are energy drains. When

we are tired, we are least likely to be objective as we process our failures and mistakes of the day. Thus the commute home can easily turn into a critical review session where your best efforts never seem good enough. In addition, news reports and irritating traffic can further deplete your energy.

Our purpose here is to help you to systematically look at daily habits that may be energy-draining, be aware of how much time is wasted on these habits, and discover some energy-producing alternatives to these habits to practice during these four maintenance periods each day.

When you answered the questions in the Action Item and added up the number of minutes you typically spend during these four time slots in your day, you probably came up with anywhere from two to four hours in which you could replace energy-sapping habits with energy builders. Let's look at some options.

One method we suggest is *combining* an activity that produces low energy for you, such as rushing to get ready for work and driving through traffic to the office, with another activity or mental strategy that will boost your energy, such as positive mental imaging or listening to calming music in the car. Then the sum of the combined activities will equal an energy gain, or at least will prevent your energy quotient from falling below par.

Many parents instinctively know the value of combining pleasant activities with unpleasant ones for their children. Anna Marie Cwieka, national account manager, The Brand Company, recalls:

"My mother was an extremely creative, right-brained person who was always finding ways to turn a negative situation into the positive for us as children. Once we had to get flu shots, so she turned the whole day into a holiday, where we secretly played hooky from school. Although we still had to get the shots, we did many other wonderful things, such as seeing a ballet in a local theater. I was truly mesmerized by it, became a ballet lover from then on, and still appreciate how my mother turned a potential ordeal into a joyful experience. I wish that, as an adult, I

*had more of my mother's adventurous attitude toward life
. . . and would [reward myself by combining] more breaks
with my daily work."*

Anna Marie is right when she says that many adults neglect to use this valuable lesson from childhood. But you can
begin combining high- and low-energy activities by turning back
to our list of five- to thirty-minute breaks in the last chapter.
Could any of them be enjoyed during your morning routine,
your commutes to and from the office, or your lunch break? Put
a check by the ones that seem most energizing to you.

Although the word "break" implies stopping one activity
and shifting to another, note that many of our energy-producing
physical and mental activities can be done while you are engaged in other activities. Thus, if right now you don't think you
can spare the extra time in the morning to exercise for twenty
minutes, you can look instead at the positive mental techniques
you can do while taking a shower and commuting to work. Try
the ideas that feel most comfortable and "do-able" to you now.

Morning Energy Maintenance

Immediately upon waking each morning, practice using the
first two to five minutes by vividly picturing your upcoming
day from start to finish in glowing positives. If it could turn
out in the best possible way, what would it look like? This
exercise is similar to making a very quick movie in your head.
(A later chapter is devoted to this mental exercise, called
"imaging.") If you find yourself falling back to sleep, do this
exercise as you get up and begin your morning routine.

Also plan something inspirational to enjoy in this initial,
attitude-setting period of your day. Because your mind is very
receptive to your feelings and ideas upon waking, whatever
you focus on sets a dominant mood for the day. Try reading a
favorite psalm or inspirational poem or enjoying music that
creates a positive mood for you. In addition, your memory is
keenest during this wake-up period. If you want to remember
some new material, reviewing it now can be much more effective than reviewing it later.

Enjoying an early brisk walk was not my life habit when I married Larry eleven years ago. In fact, then I would say (and truly believed) that I was just not a "morning person." I wasn't mentally alert until 10:00 A.M. (even though I was always up and at the office early).

But my husband, who is a dentist, lived on a very different time schedule. If I didn't get up early with him, I missed seeing and talking with him until late afternoon. So partly to enjoy the special morning time with him and partly because I suspected that it might help my energy level and general health habits, I began to get up at 5:00 A.M. and run or walk with him. Now I am amazed at the changes this has brought me. I gain four or five extra hours each day when I am mentally alert. Furthermore, my metabolism is working much more effectively, so my weight stays steady.

Next, can you make time to sit down and enjoy a healthy breakfast? Many professionals fall into the trap of gulping down their coffee and a meager slice of toast as they are dressing or driving to work. This manner of eating is not relaxing and may even provoke enough stress to interfere with digestion. Also, meals eaten on the run are rarely nutritious.

We believe, like many nutritionists, that breakfast is the most important meal of the day. Eating a high-fiber, low-sugar cereal and/or whole wheat item, fresh fruit, low-fat or skim milk, and no more than one cup of coffee or caffeinated tea is the best breakfast option for most adults. How does this compare with your normal breakfast fare?

A High-Energy Commute

Two factors can greatly enhance your energy maintenance during your daily commute to the office. First, leave home with plenty of time to spare. That means giving yourself at least fifteen minutes' leeway in case you hit a traffic jam or miss your bus or train. Then if problems do arise, you can face them calmly rather than chastising yourself about being late. Second, plan some restful, inspirational, or educational activity to do during your commute. Listen to some favorite classical music or tapes of experts in your field of business.

Your morning commute is also a great time to mentally rehearse any meetings or presentations you will be making during the day. Make your thoughts and images positive views of the events so that you are rehearsing not only your presentation but also a successful outcome (which often becomes a self-fulfilling prophecy!).

In addition, if you leave home with time to spare, chances are that you will also arrive at work a few minutes early. This extra time is a luxury, offering you a high-energy opportunity to gather your thoughts, plan both your work and joy break schedule, and move comfortably into your day.

Maintaining Energy During Lunch

For lunch, we recommend planning at least twenty to thirty minutes of positive energy-building time. If we are meeting with someone else, we have learned to suggest some topics we would like to discuss over lunch. Then we rarely get caught listening to a long tale of woe. It's fine to briefly focus on problems, but don't let it dissolve into an energy-draining complaint session. To avoid this, quickly move the topic on to positive solutions or other positive thoughts.

Remember that worry and negative thoughts don't mix well with eating. The brain creates body chemicals that counteract effective digestion when we worry, fret, argue, or process negative thoughts. So focus on the positive during meal times, and teach those you share meals with to do the same.

Before we leave the lunch-break period, let's also consider what you choose to eat for lunch. Do you ever struggle to stay alert for the two hours right after lunch? If so, chances are you made some poor food choices. Heavy food, rich in fat and cholesterol, or foods high in salt, sugar, and caffeine are poor energy choices. Rich, high-fat foods cause most of your energy to be tied up digesting your lunch for the next two hours or so. Some studies indicate that after such a meal, the blood actually becomes more viscous and has less oxygen. Or if you load up on sugar, you might be one of those people who feel the "sugar blues" for the next hour or so. As your glucose goes high to process all that sugar and then stays there, your energy will drop.

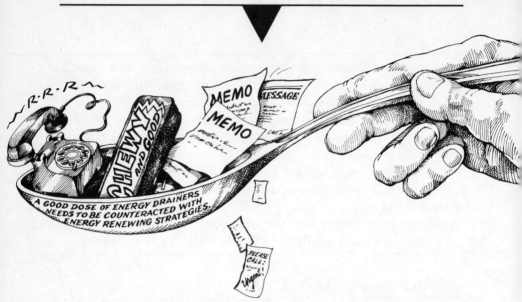

A GOOD DOSE OF ENERGY DRAINERS NEEDS TO BE COUNTERACTED WITH ENERGY RENEWING STRATEGIES.

On the other hand, if you want to have optimum energy for the afternoon, choose fresh fruits or steamed vegetables. A salad with a very light dressing or no dressing is great. Enjoy the crispness and pure flavor without all that gooey dressing. A vegetable soup, again low in salt and fat, is good. Whole-grain breads are a great source of nutrition and fiber. Learn to enjoy their taste without butter. And skip the dessert.

We may have just shot holes in one of your favorite forms of fun—eating a good old American junk-food lunch—so be gentle with yourself. And rest assured that you don't have to change a thing until or unless you want to. In fact, if you feel pressured to change, you will resist. You can make permanent, lasting change only when it is your free and self-directed choice. So if right now you don't feel ready to change any of your eating habits, trust this inner feeling and move on to other areas where you are ready to change for the better. We have found that as we get other areas of our lives in balance with other sources of pleasure besides eating, it isn't as difficult to give up poor eating habits.

Rebuilding Energy During the Commute Home

If you have been able to enjoy two to three joy breaks during your afternoon (and possibly a short catnap), you have probably been able to sustain most of your energy. You can restore your energy even more, however, by making your commute home a restful and uplifting experience. Try making a ritual out of focusing only on what you did right or well that day. The commute home is a poor time to try to be objective and to harvest any negatives or failures. It is a great time, however, just to appreciate any and all affirmative efforts you made that day. After practicing this exercise, you will be continually amazed at how many of your positive deeds and gestures you will overlook unless you make a conscious effort to take time to review and appreciate yourself. This step will help you arrive home in a cheerful frame of mind, feeling entitled to an enjoyable evening spent with yourself or your family.

Another positive activity for the commute is to mentally remind yourself of all the possible ways you could choose to enjoy parts of your evening. By planning some purposeful fun into each evening, and by making a commitment to yourself to make it happen, you will arrive home ready to enjoy the evening.

If your day has been stressful, it can feel great to take twenty minutes or more to enjoy a brisk walk, bike ride, or other aerobic exercise to get the stress toxins out of your system. If you sink into your big easy chair and doze off, you will often find that you wake up groggy, as tired or more tired than when you went to sleep. This is because toxins build up in your bloodstream and are trapped there. If you enjoy (this is an important part of the process) any form of aerobic exercise, the deep breathing and increased pumping of your heart will flush out the toxins and bring in lots of fresh, energizing oyxgen. As a result, you will be revived and ready to enjoy a pleasant evening with a good energy level.

To close this section on the four energy-maintenance times, listen to how two executives boost their energy levels during their regular work travel. Imagine if your commute involved a ten- or twelve-hour transatlantic jet flight. That's the regular "office commute" that Hugh Coble, group president of operations for Fluor Daniel, Inc., dealt with for six months while he flew back and forth between England and Fluor Daniel's various sites in the United States. Yet by incorporating relaxation techniques, high-energy eating habits, and a positive attitude into what many would term an "ordeal," he was able to hop off the plane with energy to spare:

"For nearly a year, I tallied up some 400,000 air miles flying back and forth between England and California. It would have been easy to run out of gas during that period. But I used energy-building techniques I learned in Perspective III (a whole-brained executive development program taught by Ann's team) to turn a potential negative into a positive. During each flight, I usually listened to motivational tapes or to soothing music. While the music played, I would visualize all the positives about my upcoming day at work—how great the first four hours would be, whom I wanted to see, and so on. Eventually I would become so relaxed that I would fall asleep. Then when I arrived in a new time zone, I would feel totally reoriented, totally relaxed. I also made a point of not drinking any alcohol. I mainly had water, and I always ordered either the low-calorie meals, the seafood selection, or occasionally the vegetarian meals. Using all these strategies was critical; I don't think I would have survived that year without them."

A financial leader tells how he uses his commute home to help renew his energy and leave his work behind at the office:

"I used to arrive at home feeling uptight and nervous, and it was difficult to get my mind off work. Two things helped me break the habit. First, I keep a yellow note stuck on the dash with a big plus sign. It reminds me to think about one good thing I did that day and not focus on something that didn't get done. Second, I stop by a rec center on the way home and walk thirty minutes, followed by a few laps in the pool. I use this as my transition time."

Building Breaks into Your Work Schedule

Our team has learned the long-term benefits of planning energy breaks as carefully as we plan work assignments. Once we discovered the intrinsic link between energy-reviving breaks and overall productivity and creativity, we stopped thinking of work and breaks as separate entities. Now we define them as basically one and the same—*a continuum of activities all geared toward accomplishing whatever goals we have set for ourselves that day.* Once you discover this for yourself, you will no longer think of breaks as being an indulgence or a gap in your work schedule. Nor will you feel guilty about taking time off to relax, because these short breaks will contribute as much to your efficient completion of a project as, say, arriving at work on time, having clear-cut objectives for the project, or having the proper skills to accomplish the task.

Even if you have been working quite successfully without taking breaks, you probably have not experienced the optimum level of creativity, motivation, and sustained energy that you can achieve. We feel confident in making this claim to our clients and seminar participants because few people can maintain a high energy level throughout the work day without stopping from time to time to

- switch brain hemispheres (helping to promote brain synergy and creativity),
- release tension and fatigue,
- rebuild the oxygen supply,
- recharge the neurotransmitters in the brain, and
- replenish energy reserves.

A good general tip when deciding what type of break to take at a given moment is to choose an activity, and possibly a location, that is different from your current task and site. For example:

1. If you have been sitting still, hunched over papers at your desk or glued to your phone, then stand up and stretch, take a walk down the hall and up a flight of stairs, and get your circulation going again. You could even grab a jump rope and get in a few minutes of fun, invigorating exercise.

2. If you have been doing close work, such as staring at figures or reading legal documents, stop and look out the

window at the sky, the cloud patterns, or the city's sky-line. You might also relax your eyes by closing them and doing an imaging exercise.

3. If you have been doing something that requires lots of concentration and accuracy, switch to a playful activity such as reading the comics, juggling, playing with jacks or wind-up toys, drawing a picture with crayons, or play-ing a game on the computer.

4. When you've been doing a task demanding creative think-ing, such as brainstorming, illustrating, writing advertising copy, or teaching, shift to a less taxing activity for a while, such as filing, unpacking your briefcase, or distributing files to personnel.

5. Finally, if you have been working alone for many hours, interact with someone else. Talking, laughing, and re-sponding to others' reactions is an energy lift. Converse-ly, if you've been engaged in meetings all day, having ten minutes to yourself will be very relaxing.

In a later section, the testimonies of top professionals about their favorite types of breaks and the benefits they derive will perhaps convince you of the value of breaks and inspire you to try a variety of activities. Once you realize their power to enhance overall productivity, accuracy, motivation, creativity, and problem-solving ability, you may want to pro-mote breaks—on both an individualized and a group basis—for your entire staff. Some of these examples address this idea as well. The end of the chapter will discuss the best times to schedule breaks.

Expanding Your List of Office Breaks

In the last chapter, we asked you to think of numerous five-to ten-minute breaks you could take at the office, plus some longer breaks that could be incorporated into a lunch hour. Were you able to come up with ten to fifteen ideas that truly sounded enjoyable and relaxing to you? Or were you

ACTION ITEM

List a number of longer activities (requiring two hours or more) that you do for fun and recreation.

Next create brief 5- to 10-minute ways to bring some of these interests into the work environment—such as sharing photos from a recent vacation or simply browsing through a golf magazine.

stumped after three or four ideas?

One tip that might help you add to your list of short breaks is to name activities you enjoy doing that require two or more hours. As we commented earlier, when most adults are asked what they consider to be their personal "play," they list activities like tennis, golf, bridge, movies, dancing, sightseeing, going to the beach, or visiting a museum.

Since the two-hour activities you list in the Action Item represent established interests, they are good sources from which to create related but shorter breaks. For example, let's say that your list includes playing tennis and golf, going to antique sales and auctions, and touring museums. Then bring your copies of *Tennis* or *Golf Digest* to work and spend a number of short breaks reading the articles in them. Or bring your putter and a few golf balls to enjoy when you have ten minutes to practice during a lunch or afternoon break.

In addition, you could bring to work a variety of books and magazines devoted to antique collecting, then leaf through them as you help yourself to a cup of herbal tea. You could also do an imaging exercise based on a past or future visit to an auction, or call up a friend and plan an antique-hunting expedition for an upcoming weekend. And to build energy based on your passion for art shows, try bringing to work colorful art books, brochures and catalogs from exhibits you have toured, biographies of your favorite artists, and articles on upcoming exhibits. If you work near a gallery or museum, you could pack a sack lunch and visit a new exhibit.

Do you see how easy it is to bring your weekend recreation and play time into the office with you? Still other types of breaks, such as imaging, taking a coffee break with a friend at the office, calling a friend on the phone, or sending a quick note to an out-of-town friend, require no extra supplies. Since we're strong advocates of variety, though, we suggest that you have an array of break-taking possibilities handy at the office.

Peak Performers' Favorite Breaks

Eleanor Roosevelt's schedule was always packed full. In addition to her duties as the wife of a prominent politician and later first lady, she always maintained a full load of personal concerns and interests. She taught school, wrote a regular newspaper column, and campaigned for issues that were close to her heart. To relax from her hectic schedule, she took brief sojourns in the country. Mrs. Roosevelt found peace and solace in rural surroundings—even if only for a short picnic between speaking engagements. When she could escape for a few days, she traveled to her country home or toured with friends. After her time in the country, she returned renewed and refreshed to the demands of her urban life.

Malcolm Forbes always combined business with pleasure. He managed to find a way to make his fun profitable. Giving elaborate parties, collecting, and motorcycle riding were all expressions of his sense of fun—and he managed to turn a profit with all of them. Striving for publicity for his magazine, he combined his enjoyment of motorcycle riding with a publicity stunt in which he dressed up a bunch of businessmen as bikers and rode them through the streets of New York. He also garnered as much publicity as he could in the course of amassing a huge collection of art, Fabergé creations, and toy soldiers.

Clarence Darrow, the famous Chicago attorney best known for his defense in the Scopes trial, spent long hours preparing his cases but found release from tension through reading. He read widely in fields that bore little relation to his work as a trial lawyer. His biographer, Irving Stone, says: "For him study was never work, but the highest of all pleasures. He liked to acquire knowledge not only because it would be useful, but because the achievement of any knowledge was sheer intellectual delight." Darrow took quick breaks throughout the day to peruse books and magazines. He read for fun and picked up anything that interested and charmed him. In the evenings, he would often invite friends into his home to share an evening of reading. He loved reading something aloud and then discussing it.

The late Isaac Asimov, one of America's most prolific writers, wrote books in almost every genre possible. He wrote on pure science, biblical scholarship, mystery, science fiction, and dozens of other topics. He loved his work and found pleasure in writing books, but he also enjoyed breaks from his writing. He called himself a "confirmed movie addict" and reported in his autobiography that he liked adventure movies and "would see, with pleasure, almost anything with swordplay or with a chase series. And I liked comedy, the more slapstick the better, and musical comedies too. . . . I didn't like what were called 'science fiction' movies." Those were too much like work and not up to his critical standards for the genre. Escape into comedy and thrillers, on the other hand, completely removed him from the work he was doing.

Mary Kay Ash, founder of Mary Kay Cosmetics, is another performer who loves her work. She says that enthusiasm was the key to her success and that when her enthusiasm slumped, she took a break to listen to motivational tapes or read motivational books. She also found singing to be a real restorer of energy. She encouraged her employees to sing at work and at home. She remembered from her years of churchgoing that the singing was always her favorite part and made her ready to listen to the message that came afterward.

Perhaps no one has more stress, more demands, and a more tightly packed schedule than the president of the United States, yet most presidents have recognized the necessity for joy breaks. Harry Truman loved plays and playing the piano and found time for both in spite of his schedule. His piano playing became a legend during his presidency.

Hearing how other peak performers, many of whom participated in our field research, spend their break times will also give you some novel suggestions for breaks. Some of these professionals had been taking breaks for years before we met them—they intuitively understood the need for refueling their energy reserves throughout the day and evening. Other managers and CEOs began after hearing our strong sales pitch on the value of energy breaks. Most of them have shared their new, high-energy routine with their staff, making breaks and toys in the office an established habit.

Vince Kontny, president of Fluor Daniel, Inc., has this to say about breaks:

> *"My main form of break-taking is merely allowing myself to daydream, letting my mind flow on to some other topic. I also enjoy looking out my window; it has a great vista of the green hills of Southern California. I have always intuitively done this, but before Ann explained the benefits of breaks, I used to feel guilty. Now I don't. My general philosophy is to approach business as a bit of a game. People frequently take things too seriously at work, so I try at times to put things in a more informal setting, such as breaking people up into teams for discussing ideas. I also try to tell some jokes during our meetings. In fact, humor is the last thing I would like to lose in my life."*

Patsy Fulton, chancellor of Oakland Community College, shares these ideas:

"I have a toybox with an assortment of energy toys in my office—a bola paddle [ball on a string], a dart board, sunglasses with pop-out eyes, and a kazoo. My collection began several years ago when my staff organized a group picnic. We decided to add extra fun to the event by bringing toys to hand out. I received the bola paddle. We organized a kazoo band and bola competitions. Now, whenever I finish with a frustrating meeting or situation, I close my door and get out that paddle to relieve stress and recover my energy.

I also believe in spreading playfulness and creative thinking throughout the office. For example, I have given all my staff a kaleidoscope, asking them to shake it up whenever they feel stuck to see the world and their problems differently. My staff also has a Fun and Games Committee that organizes an appreciation day each semester when we hand out ribbons and balloons and have special events together. You have to remember to have fun together, to break the tension and enjoy that other side of each other's personality."

Paul Varello, chairman and CEO of American REF-FUEL, also takes energy breaks:

"If I'm working on a tough, left-brained job and my mental energy is draining, I shift for a while into thinking about one of my creative projects at home. I will doodle out my ideas for the next step on the project and consider different options I might have. Then I can go back to my left-brained project fully charged with energy. It works every time.

If I have a whole Saturday at home (not often the case), I'll spend half an hour just walking around my workshop and house finding the jobs I think I'd like to do that day, such as building a clock, fixing a faucet, adding a planter, or painting a bird feeder. Then that's what I do. By the end of the weekend I'm fully recharged and ready for my left-brained working world!"

Angela Ozymy, an administrative assistant with Martin Insurance Agency, describes a successful break at her company:

"Last spring the people in our office decided to take a group break together, a picnic during the lunch hour. We also decided it would be fun to relive some of our child-hood days. First of all, we dressed in the garb we enjoyed wearing in school, then did things that were popular back then, such as jacks, jump rope, bubble blowing, and fris-bee throwing. We also played 'do you remember when?' There was 100 percent participation in all activities. At the end of the picnic, everyone's energy level had increased, people had smiles on their faces, and there was very little friction between people for the rest of the afternoon regardless of the problems we were involved in. This extended joy break worked!"

As you can see, breaks come in a variety of shapes and forms for different peak performers. Virtually anything that diverts your mind from the work at hand and gives you a few minutes of humor, relaxation, pleasure, sensory stimulation, exercise, and just plain fun will give you an energy boost. In addition, many professionals use a wooden foot roller, a hand exerciser, or a tactile toy like a koosh ball to ease fatigue as they talk business on the phone.

But let me interject here that, just as children frequently grow bored with their toys, adults can be expected to feel the same way. Remember that change, novelty, and surprise are all powerful suppliers of mental energy. So switch your energy toys and routines from time to time. Every few months, take yourself to a novelty shop or all-ages toy store and see what piques your fancy. Then put that dart board away for a few months and replace it with a game of ring toss or a beautiful puzzle that you can enjoy for five minutes between tasks.

Tips on Scheduling Breaks

Now that you have a multitude of suggestions for types of breaks to take, let's consider when to schedule those energy lifts. Some days, due to your workload, your mental set, or your physical condition, you may feel the need to take a short break every hour or so. At other times you may have enough momentum to concentrate on a project for two to three hours before you need a break. And sometimes your agenda may be so tightly packed that your break may merely consist of taking a series of deep, slow breaths between appointments.

In general, we encourage taking an average of two short breaks in the morning and two in the afternoon. But if you are a "morning person" and naturally have much more energy before noon than after, you may prefer to take just one break in the morning and three to four in the afternoon. If you are an "evening person," just the opposite may be true for you. Obviously, scheduling breaks is a highly individualistic thing, and you will probably want to experiment to find out when, and under what circumstances, you will benefit most by taking a cleansing, energy-reviving break.

In addition, asking yourself a few questions about your natural energy highs and lows will help you determine other times when a break is in order. First, notice which of your regular projects make you feel least motivated and which tend to drain your energy. Slotting a break at the start and finish of these tasks can balance a low-energy task with two high-energy activities. Furthermore, as mentioned above, you may feel the need to take more breaks during your low-energy periods when your energy tends to sag (such as after lunch).

Another time to schedule a break is after dealing with an energy-sapping personality. Simply being in the presence of these pessimistic, gloom-and-doom types can drain your energy. On the other hand, having a visit with an optimistic, motivated person will give you an energy boost. You can use these people as sources of breaks for you—in a phone conversation, a coffee break, a lunch date, or a shared work project. In fact, talking to a high-energy person after experiencing a low-energy personality is another good energy strategy.

We also encourage taking breaks connected with six fairly common conditions: lack of motivation, tension, high-concentration work, procrastination, complex work, and mental blocks.

1. **Lack of motivation.** When your motivation is waning or you can no longer make a decision on something mundane, take a short break. Granted, sometimes you are working on such a tight schedule that you feel unable to spare even five minutes. But when you notice yourself

   ■ having to reread the same material twice because nothing sank in the first time,
   ■ daydreaming and staring out the window,
   ■ feeling so restless that you want to climb out the window, and
   ■ making careless errors,

   you are not working up to speed anyway and are already squandering your time by working very inefficiently. It is much better to simply put down your work for a moment and recharge your batteries. We suggest that you get up from wherever you are, stretch, take some deep breaths, and immerse yourself in a totally different activity that will engage your other brain hemisphere and bring you some instant pleasure. If you are feeling sleepy, a brisk walk around the block (or up several flights of stairs) will help to jump-start your metabolism and fill your brain with oxygen. Doing something that piques your emotions—that makes you chuckle or feel happy—will also give you an emotional energy boost. You might try something that will build both physical and mental energy, such as juggling, playing with a yo-yo, or waltzing around the office to some music.

2. **Tension.** Whenever you feel tense, frustrated, or angry, it's also time for a break. Of course, heading for the gym for a good workout is the most thorough way to release stress and the toxins it produces in your body. But short of that, taking any kind of break that refocuses your attention on something positive will help. Doing several minutes of deep breathing and positive imaging is one effective type of stress breaker. During your imaging, take yourself to a place that connotes utter peace and sensual pleasure to you. During this exercise, you can physically unwind by

contracting all your muscles, starting from your toes and working up to your face, then releasing them.

Laughter is another powerful tension breaker. Call a friend or colleague and, instead of sharing your frustrations, get away from the situation by sharing some laughs.

3. **High-concentration work.** Are you engaged in work that requires memorization or the analysis of new information? Some studies indicate that memory is highest at the beginning and end of each work period. So several shorter work or study periods can be far more effective than one long, unbroken period. For most folks, an hour is the maximum amount of time that the brain can take in new data before needing time to stop and process it. By shifting your attention to an entirely different activity—preferably one that stimulates your opposite brain hemisphere—you allow your brain to process and store this collection of new information.

4. **Procrastination.** We advise using breaks as a reward for completing a project. Having a special lunch or energy break to look forward to will help sustain your momentum as you work on your assignment. Or if it is an unpleasant but necessary task for which you can drum up almost no enthusiasm, use a reward at the close of the project to serve as your source of motivation.

5. **Complex work.** Breaks can help you to separate a long, complex assignment into a series of "do-able" steps. For example, if you are asked to create a three-year projected budget for your division, the task at first may seem so laborious and time-consuming that the mere thought of beginning makes you tired. Rather than procrastinating until the last minute, try to break the job down into ten one-hour steps that you schedule over several days and that are followed up by ten fun, rewarding breaks. The assignment will feel less overwhelming.

6. **Mental blocks.** Whenever you feel stumped and are unable to come up with the answer to a problem you've

been trying to solve, that's another clear-cut signal that a break is needed. In this case, a longer break is usually necessary. Sometimes your subconscious mind needs a night's sleep to dwell on the problem and come up with the creative breakthrough. Sometimes an activity that will clear your mind of all work-related data, such as a game of tennis, a movie, or time spent with your kids, will enable your mind to hit upon the answer you are seeking. Staying at your desk and trying to browbeat yourself into coming up with the solution will rarely bring you the desired results. Your time will be much better spent by taking a break to switch gears, then refocusing on another assignment for the rest of the day.

The few minutes you put your work aside to take a break will pay off in the extra productivity you will gain by not letting your energy dwindle as the afternoon and evening go by. Just think of how much time it takes to reread several pages of a report that you daydreamed through, to rewrite a poorly composed letter, to refigure a column of expenses that you miscalculated, or to apologize to an employee you snapped at because you were tired and frustrated. Our list of examples could go on and on simply by taking them from our own lives during the times we functioned at a below-average level because we allowed our energy reserves to run low. So whenever you think you don't have time for a break, weigh the probable consequences and the time required to correct them.

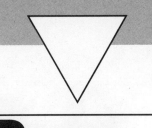

CHAPTER

BRAIN DOMINANCE AND ENERGY:

What's Good About Your Messy Desk?

66When I eat a tomato I look at it the way anyone else would. But when I paint a tomato, then I see it differently. **99**

—Matisse in Gertrude Stein, *Picasso*

66When the 'weaker' of the two brains [is] stimulated and encouraged to work in cooperation with the stronger side, the end result [is] a great increase in overall ability and . . . often five to ten times more effectiveness. **99**

—Professor Robert Ornstein, University of California

n Chapter 3 you learned about fifteen behavior traits that produce high energy levels in children and you observed these tendencies in the outstanding role models for high energy that were profiled. We have also found and studied these same behavioral traits among the highly accomplished men and women we have taught and worked with. Thus we are convinced of the link between these actions and high energy output.

Yet these behavior traits are not the most fundamental source of energy stimulation and maintenance. Underlying the external actions are four integral mental principles that are the real basis of ongoing Energy Engineering. They are

- working and living in sync with your brain dominance;

- balancing both brain hemispheres through brain integration rather than mental duality;

- creating and experiencing a balanced blend of work and play throughout the day and the week; and

- experiencing a stimulating, pleasing work environment that supports your brain dominance.

For most of us adults, the ability to continually rebuild our energy reserves—doing it so naturally and efficiently that we rarely suffer a major eɪ.ergy setback unless an illness sets in—requires a fine-tuned balancing act. Like learning to ski or ride a bike, balancing energy loss and gain requires practice and foresight. Mastering these four mental principles is well worth the effort, however, because they can produce the kind of drive, vitality, and achievement levels that you observed in the six high-energy role models profiled in Chapter 3. These four principles can also make burnout and most illness a thing of the past, for many illnesses occur when we have blocked or overstimulated our immune system by living out of balance for long periods.

This chapter will discuss how and why these four principles build energy.

Discovering Your Brain Dominance and Its Link to Energy

One of the most effective steps you can take to quickly increase your energy is to discover your natural brain dominance, then to develop a work style that is in sync with it. The term "brain dominance" refers to a person's tendency to think and act according to the characteristics of one side, or hemisphere, of the brain cortex rather than the other side. Over the past thirty years, Roger Sperry, Robert Ornstein, and other scientists have learned a great deal about the individual traits of the brain's two frontal hemispheres. We are beginning to understand how brain dominances affect our behavior, our learning and work styles, and our personalities.

One of the first indications of the separate functioning of the brain's two hemispheres occurred when physicians discovered that an injury to the left side produced very different results than an injury to the right side did. The left side appears to govern the ability to use language, writing, and mathematics; to perform logical deductions and other types of analysis; and to be disciplined. The right side of the brain appears to govern visual, spatial, artistic, and intuitive concepts and to be the source of imagination and spontaneous play. Persons who have suffered either a stroke or a damaging blow to the left side of their brain, for example, often are unable to put their thoughts into words (speech and writing). Yet they are able to draw pictures to convey their ideas.

In the early 1960s Roger Sperry began research that confirmed the two hemispheres' separate functions, earning him a Nobel Prize in 1983. In one experiment he studied the brains of epileptic patients in whom the connection between left and right hemispheres had been severed in order to decrease the symptoms of their disease. A split-brain patient held a pencil in his right hand but was not allowed to see it. Because the right hand is connected to the left brain hemisphere, the patient could describe it in words. But when he held a pencil in the opposite hand, which stimulated the right brain hemisphere, he could not identify it by speech but could only point to a picture of it.

Despite some controversy on the matter, the latest research conducted on brain hemispheres firmly acknowledges the differences between the two sides and their functions. Experiments indicate that several areas of the left brain are engaged in reading language, and with new technology, we can now be more specific and pinpoint where the left brain processes rhyming words, the meaning of words, and familiar words. It is now possible to track any task being performed by the brain and know its location.

Before we describe some of the separate characteristics of the two sides, first realize that there is a constant give and take between the right and left hemispheres of a normal brain. The two hemispheres are connected by a bundle of nerve fibers called the corpus callosum, which serves as an instant message pathway. Therefore, the two sides are constantly "in touch" with each other. In addition, many abilities such as writing a poem or performing in a play require the continual cooperation of both sides of the brain, because both activities need an emotional and aesthetic response as well as logic, analysis, and language skills.

However, certain tasks and responses are thought to primarily require the work of one side of the brain more than the other. In addition, most of us develop a preferred, or dominant, side of the brain. The more that we call on, and thus stimulate, this preferred hemisphere, the better it performs for us and the more we depend on it. In this way, developing a brain dominance is similar to being left- or right-handed and choosing to do things like write, throw, and eat with the dominant hand. The more skilled we become with our dominant hand, the clumsier and more unacceptable becomes the performance of the other hand, and we stop developing certain skills with it. In the same way we seem to develop a brain hemisphere dominance.

This can cause problems when we are faced with situations where new skills and thinking patterns are needed. Professor Robert Ornstein of the University of California found that "people who have been trained to use one side of their brain more or less exclusively were relatively unable to use the other side, both in general and in those situations where the activities specifically related to the other side were needed." Even if you have come to rely heavily on only one side of your brain, there is always the opportunity to change. Professor Ornstein continues:

> *"When the 'weaker' of the two brains was stimulated and encouraged to work in cooperation with the stronger side, the end result was a great increase in overall ability and effectiveness. Actual results showed that the brain can sometimes work in a way different from the standard mathematics (1 side + 1 side = twice as effective performance), for when one side was 'added' to the other side, the results were often five to ten times more effectiveness."*

The exercise entitled "Self-Assessment of Brain Dominance and Energy" will help you identify your natural brain dominance as it links to ways you gain or lose energy.

Recognizing your current brain hemisphere profile is a great opportunity for you to make major energy gains. Duality and integration will be described in the next chapter. Unlimited energy comes from learning to call on both hemispheres in balance as supportive partners. This is a basic key to high energy.

Self-Assessment of Brain Dominance and Energy

Read through the following list of statements and quickly decide which tasks give you energy and which drain your energy. Circle the number that best represents your energy response to the task. The scale ranges from "5" (for a task or behavior that highly energizes you) to "–5" (for a task that leaves you energy-depleted).

If you find that on some statements you have both responses (sometimes you get energy from this situation and sometimes it drains your energy), then score twice on that line, once for the degree of energy gain and once for the degree of energy drain.

1. I enjoy and get energy from creating options such as making "to-do" lists, brainstorming possible places to go on vacation, thinking of many ways to do a project. In meetings, I can get interested in a new idea and get energy by adding lots of ideas to it.

◀ Energy Gain   5 4 3 2 1 0 –1 –2 –3 –4 –5   Energy Drain ▶

(Remember to score on both sides if you sometimes gain energy and sometimes lose energy from the same activity.)

2. I get energy from creating order and organizing. I enjoy going through piles of stuff and eliminating the unnecessary. In meetings, I get energy by bringing agenda items to closure and knowing that specific tasks are assigned and will be followed up.

◀ Energy Gain   5 4 3 2 1 0 –1 –2 –3 –4 –5   Energy Drain ▶

3. I get my creative juices going by having all my materials out to work with. Typically I have lots of stuff around me in my work area.

◀ Energy Gain   5 4 3 2 1 0 –1 –2 –3 –4 –5   Energy Drain ▶

4. I typically leave my desk and work area straight and clean primarily because I get energy from putting things back in their place and like to work in a clean, neat area. This seems to apply equally to projects at home such as yard work.

◀ Energy Gain   5 4 3 2 1 0 –1 –2 –3 –4 –5   Energy Drain ▶

5. I enjoy and get energized by juggling several tasks at once and by moving from one to the other intuitively. As I tire of one job or get blocked on how to proceed, I shift and work awhile on another task. This is energizing for me and I often get ideas for one project by putting it out of my mind and working on something completely different.

◀ Energy Gain   5 4 3 2 1 0 –1 –2 –3 –4 –5   Energy Drain ▶

6. I get energy by finishing one thing before I move on to the next. I prefer to create and follow an orderly process in my work. I accomplish high-priority tasks first and then move on to lower priorities.

◀ Energy Gain   5 4 3 2 1 0 –1 –2 –3 –4 –5   Energy Drain ▶

7. I seem to get energy from being unpredictable. I like to keep all my options open and find being flexible and spontaneous easy and energizing.

◀ Energy Gain   5 4 3 2 1 0 –1 –2 –3 –4 –5   Energy Drain ▶

8. I get energy from being predictable and want others to do the same for me. I enjoy planning and keeping on schedule, and knowing well in advance what is coming.

◀ Energy Gain   5 4 3 2 1 0 –1 –2 –3 –4 –5   Energy Drain ▶

9. I get energy from breaking old rules and policies and finding new ways to get things done. I frequently find rules and policies limiting.

◀ Energy Gain   5 4 3 2 1 0 –1 –2 –3 –4 –5   Energy Drain ▶

10. I prefer to follow the rules and wish others would as well. For me, policies and structure help things to run consistently smoothly. I get energy by providing a positive role model for "going by the book."

◀ Energy Gain   5 4 3 2 1 0 –1 –2 –3 –4 –5   Energy Drain ▶

11. I get energy by risking. I seem to leave things until the last minute and frequently race to meet an important deadline or have to rush in traffic to get places on time. Racing in just at the eleventh hour seems to give me a rush of adrenaline. I perform well under pressure so I don't worry about this part of my profile.

◀ Energy Gain   5 4 3 2 1 0 –1 –2 –3 –4 –5   Energy Drain ▶

12. I get energy by planning ahead in detail and allowing a safety "cushion" of time so that I won't lose energy by getting pressured into a mad rush at the last minute. I pride myself on being prompt and usually am early to most appointments and meetings.

◀ Energy Gain   5   4   3   2   1   0   −1   −2   −3   −4   −5   Energy Drain ▶

13. I get energy by "flying by the seat of my pants" on projects and other assignments. When specifications are too detailed, there is not as much opportunity for me to get into it and innovate. I prefer a wide-open assignment and enjoy the challenge of a spur-of-the-moment need to respond without lots of planning or rehearsal.

◀ Energy Gain   5   4   3   2   1   0   −1   −2   −3   −4   −5   Energy Drain ▶

14. I prefer to plan and rehearse. I want to have a clear idea of what I am going to do and what is expected of me well before the deadline. "Flying by the seat of my pants" is not my best style. I get energy by having the time to coordinate my plans with others.

◀ Energy Gain   5   4   3   2   1   0   −1   −2   −3   −4   −5   Energy Drain ▶

15. I get energy by tackling the impossible. The bigger the challenge, the more I like it. In fact, when things get too easy I may even subconsciously cause a little crisis just to keep things stirred up.

◀ Energy Gain   5   4   3   2   1   0   −1   −2   −3   −4   −5   Energy Drain ▶

16. I get energy by implementing solutions. Once a new project has been conceptualized, my strong suit is to manage the project to completion.

◀ Energy Gain   5   4   3   2   1   0   −1   −2   −3   −4   −5   Energy Drain ▶

17. I do my research, but I trust my intuition and get energy by leaving things a bit open. I like to go into a situation without too much preconditioning so my intuition can work. For example, in a sales call or project negotiation, I trust my ability to listen to and read the client and respond in the moment, so I don't do a lot of rehearsal and tight planning prior to the event.

◀ Energy Gain   5   4   3   2   1   0   −1   −2   −3   −4   −5   Energy Drain ▶

18. I get energy by researching all the options before starting. I probably put more time than most into planning and research, but this is my strong suit and I enjoy this part of the job.

◀ Energy Gain   5   4   3   2   1   0   −1   −2   −3   −4   −5   Energy Drain ▶

19. I get energy with a new challenge. I find myself more challenged if I move on to a new job or position every three years or so. For me the big energy comes at the beginning when I am trying to get on top of the assignment and see the big picture. Once I have the job in hand, I find myself looking for a new challenge.

◀ Energy Gain   5   4   3   2   1   0   −1   −2   −3   −4   −5   Energy Drain ▶

20. I get energy when I've been at a job long enough to reach mastery. I like to stay with a job at least five to seven years. I feel that I do my best work in a new assignment after I've learned the ropes.

◀ Energy Gain   5   4   3   2   1   0   −1   −2   −3   −4   −5   Energy Drain ▶

Now go back and total your scores on the odd-numbered questions (1, 3, 5, 7, 9, etc.) for energy gains ____ and energy drains____. These questions describe more right-brained processes, so if you have a high energy-gain score here (and a low energy-drain score), most likely you are a dominant right-brained person. Next, total your scores on the even-numbered questions (2, 4, 6, 8, etc.) for energy gains _____ and energy drains _____. These describe a classic left-brained preference. Thus, if you have high energy-gain scores for these questions and low energy drains, very likely your mental processing is dominant left-brain. And what if your scores seem balanced with energy gains from both odd- and even-numbered answers? If most of your energy-gain scores are high, you probably have already discovered your own ways of using your two hemispheres as supportive partners. We call this profile *brain integration*. However, if you use both systems represented by the twenty questions but still end most days feeling drained or wiped out, then you may be using both hemispheres but one against the other—a process called *duality*.

Brain Dominance and Work Styles

If you behave one way at work and another way at home, your behavior at home may be the most natural way for you to act because you are freer to act more in accordance with your feelings than you probably are at work. This behavior is the most likely indicator of your real brain dominance. Many people at our seminars who initially thought they were left-brained because of the work habits they followed at the office discovered that they exhibited strong right-brained tendencies once they were away from work. In these cases they are probably either right-brain dominant or, if they feel fairly comfortable both at home and at work, they have learned to balance both sides of their brain and thus are whole-brained.

To begin to analyze what these results can tell you about your natural—rather than imposed—work style, briefly review the key characteristics of your brain dominance found in the two lists. People with left-brained preferences usually process information in a manner that is sequential and logical. They prefer to deal with concrete data (rather than nebulous or unstructured information), rules, systems, linear processes, and mathematical and written problems. They also like to work in a step-by-step fashion and to complete one project before going on to another—a monochrome approach to time. They thrive on consistency; thus they often get frustrated if their plans and daily schedules are changed or interrupted. They dislike clutter and prefer keeping their work in neat, organized areas or filed away when not in use. In addition, they usually prefer to work alone in a quiet setting. Traditional time management principles are suited for left-brained folks who are good at planning, establishing priorities, and scheduling their daily tasks, then staying focused on their agenda. These people are primarily convergent thinkers, those who prefer to narrow down options, stay focused on priorities, and eliminate the extraneous.

Conversely, right-brain-oriented people are energized by a different set of conditions. They usually find inflexible routines to be boring or stifling. Thus they enjoy change, flexible schedules, working spontaneously and intuitively, taking on

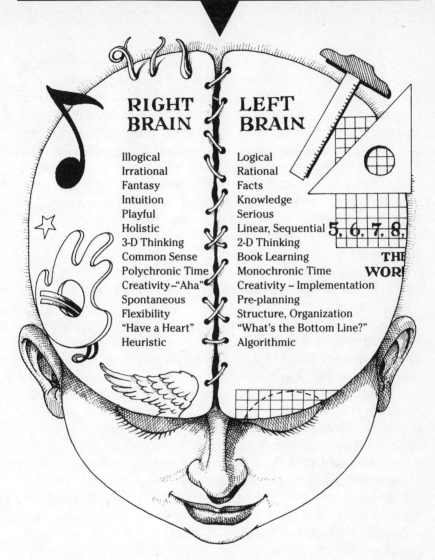

RIGHT BRAIN

Illogical
Irrational
Fantasy
Intuition
Playful
Holistic
3-D Thinking
Common Sense
Polychronic Time
Creativity–"Aha"
Spontaneous
Flexibility
"Have a Heart"
Heuristic

LEFT BRAIN

Logical
Rational
Facts
Knowledge
Serious
Linear, Sequential
2-D Thinking
Book Learning
Monochronic Time
Creativity – Implementation
Pre-planning
Structure, Organization
"What's the Bottom Line?"
Algorithmic

new challenges, and working on several projects during the day. Since they usually prefer a polychronic time frame—dealing with many things at the same time—they work well under a tight schedule (which is why many of them let projects go until the last minute) and get energized by challenging or unconventional situations. Most like to have lots of sensory stimulation within their work area, including bright colors, posters, and other kinds of artwork and music. They also like to have their work within view, which accounts for the large stacks of folders, papers, and equipment that are found in most right-brain-oriented work spaces. In fact, having these constant visual cues about what they are working on now, and what they intend to get to next week, reminds them to keep incubating ideas and makes them feel much more comfortable and secure than filing their work away out of view. Furthermore, many right-brained people complain that when they file their work, they often can't recall which heading they filed it under and end up with several file folders for the same project, all under different headings. This is most likely a result of their being strongly divergent thinkers. They are very good at creating a wide variety of options, but not as good as convergent thinkers at being consistent. As a result, they might file their home insurance papers under "H" for home, "I" for insurance, "P" for policy, "F" for fire, or "J" for the Jim Dandy Insurance Company.

Right-brained people also tend to be very inventive and imaginative folks who need time to dwell upon their formative ideas and work plans. Many are adroit problem solvers who can come up with a variety of alternatives to a situation. They are better at conceptualizing the whole picture rather than remembering to attend to all the details involved. They approach projects intuitively and may be more open about and influenced by their emotions than left-brained people.

Professions that are mainly suited to right-brained people include the arts and entertaining, teaching, writing, decorating, architecture, counseling, motivational speaking, advertising and marketing, sales, and the ministry. Professions that primarily (but certainly not exclusively) attract left-brained people are engineering, accounting, research, law, computer technology, and science.

However, there are many exceptions to the description above. In working with a large majority of engineers as clients (almost all men), our team has discovered that there are a significant number who are what we call "closet right-brain dominant." We playfully gave them this name because, although they have learned to give the impression through their work methods and behaviors that they are dominant left-brained, in truth it is their right-brained skills and traits that work the best for them.

Typically these engineers are strongly visual, work on several projects at once, moving from one to another as needed, and are strongly intuitive, but can mask their decisions in enough data to convince others that they get their answers analytically (when actually they are working backward—intuitively deciding what needs to happen and then collecting the facts to support their intuition).

John Reed is CEO of Citicorp, the largest bank in the country and perhaps the most powerful bank in the world. Typically, bankers are left-brained, conservative, and careful. Reed is none of these things. Of himself, Reed says, "I am a natural child." In a profile for *Manhattan, Inc.,* Suzanna Andrews says, "Reed is a maverick. His laugh is raucous and infectious; too loud, some complain—too free—for the power he holds." Throughout his career in banking, he has taken chances, given free rein to his playful self, and scored win after win for his bank. One of his co-workers comments, "Johnny sees things from a different perspective," and Reed agrees. He says that he puts great stock in intuition and takes his own and that of other people seriously. He also is very sensitive to the mood of people and places and has a great appreciation for beautiful things. Andrews describes Reed's management style as a willingness to try things and says that the bank is "a loosely structured corporation ruled by a chaotic kind of creativity." The bank is a place where ideas are tested, and the emphasis is on customer satisfaction rather than the bottom line. Reed says, "I'm not one of those rigorous people. I change. I learn. I'm an evolving complex system." And he laughs as he says it.

The right-brained polychronic person is more apt to focus on people's feelings, a lack of group consensus, and side issues that are obstructing a cooperative spirit. These complex issues are unpredictable in advance, so polychronic people frequently go beyond preset time lines.

In contrast, left-brained monochronic people focus on preset agendas, schedules, and deadlines. People issues and in-the-moment new ideas are more apt to be seen as interruptions and unnecessary tangents. The priority is to stay on schedule and to be punctual.

Of course, both types of brain dominance are equally valuable and necessary in this world. What matters is that you learn to work in sync with your natural dominance—which is the most productive and energy-efficient way for each individual to work—while respecting and supporting those with an opposite brain dominance. Learning how to be whole-brained—how to integrate both hemispheres into a harmonious working relationship—is the next high-energy building block. This step necessitates learning to respect your less dominant hemisphere and allowing it to affect your ideas and behavior. In addition to increasing your energy, you will become a more well-rounded person, able to meet a wider range of challenges in your job and life.

Stimulants and "Tools" for Both Brain Hemispheres

Another way to understand what produces and drains your energy is to think about stimulants and/or "tools" for each brain hemisphere. We've listed some below.

Right-Brained Preferences

- New things to explore
- Sensory stimuli: beautiful objects, pleasing sounds and smells, interesting colors, shapes, and textures
- Fun activities: toys, games, fanciful objects
- Free emotional expression (feelings of joy, excitement, fear, anger, caring)
- Interactions with others
- Being surrounded with work (or hobbies); having things in view
- Things that produce laughter

Left-Brained Preferences

- Familiar objects and procedures
- Tools, equipment, and other things that are considered useful
- Logical progression of facts
- Rules, systems
- Approaching things rationally; being in control of feelings
- Quiet and solitude
- Neat, organized; work filed away out of sight
- Activities construed as productive and serious

Working and Thinking Styles

In addition to having a preference for different stimulants and objects, the two hemispheres prefer very different ways of thinking, learning, working, and being.

Right-Brained Preferences	Left-Brained Preferences
■ "Cluttered" desk and office; things out in view	■ Tidy and organized; things out of sight
■ Enjoying new challenges and risks	■ Predictable situations; knowing what's coming
■ Jumping from project to project or juggling several things at once before going on to the next	■ Working in a step-by-step style; finishing one project before starting the next
■ Considering or experimenting with many options (may seem disorderly or indecisive to a left-brained person)	■ Sticking to one plan (creating "order")
■ Being flexible and sometimes unpredictable	■ Following set procedure; predictable, dependable
■ Last-minute projects and "flying by the seat of the pants"; often putting off finishing something, incubating options and ideas, until the final deadline	■ Detailed planning; sticking to a schedule; avoiding the risk of leaving things to the last minute
■ Conceptualizing	■ Following plans; completing projects
■ Frequently acting playful or emotional; may work sporadically rather than methodically	■ More often working seriously, methodically, steadily
■ Breaking or bending rules	■ Following rules
■ Divergent thinking	■ Convergent thinking

In an interview with *Forbes,* Masaru Ibuka, cofounder and honorary chairman of Sony, attributed his company's phenomenal success to never following the others. He looks for innovative employees at major universities, but, he says, he doesn't necessarily pick top students. "I never had much use for specialists. Specialists are inclined to argue why you can't do something, while our emphasis has always been to make something out of nothing." Sony releases 1,000 new products a year created by "nonspecialists."

Synergy—The Biphasic or Balanced Option

Stephen Covey, in *The Seven Habits of Highly Effective People,* stated: "Synergy is the essence of principle-centered leadership. It is the essence of principle-centered parenting. It catalyzes, unifies, and unleashes the greatest powers within people. The essence of synergy is to value differences—to respect them, to build on strengths, to compensate for weaknesses."

People who have developed whole-brain integration (synergy) are those who are able to combine what appear to be opposites within their personalities and habits. They choose not to follow one strict path, but to select their behavior in response to each individual situation. Psychologist Al Siebert has studied survivors of many different kinds of crises and has discovered that one of their most prominent characteristics is the ability to meld many opposites. He calls these "biphasic traits." The people who do well in crisis situations are those who can be both: serious and playful, tough and gentle, logical and intuitive, hard-working and lazy, shy and aggressive, introspective and outgoing, encouraging and demanding, supportive and confrontational, and so on. They are people who are flexible enough to respond to many different situations in a variety of ways. And, because they use all parts of their brain, they have a wide array of resources to draw from.

Discovering your initial brain dominance (if you do not yet have a balanced, "whole-brained" orientation) is the first step toward creating a harmonious interchange between your two hemispheres. The next step is understanding how this dominance affects your organizational, learning, and overall work patterns and then creating a comfortable and energy-efficient work style for yourself. This step is crucial, because working out of sync with your natural brain dominance is like trying to walk with your shoes on the wrong feet or trying to write with the opposite hand from the one you are used to. In other words, it feels uncomfortable, jarring, frustrating, and tiring. And it requires a much greater expenditure of energy.

For example, a left-brained person most likely would feel uncomfortable if she were suddenly transferred into an office space occupied by two right-brained work partners. The left-brained worker probably would prefer to work in silence at a neat work area. She would feel best starting each project well in advance of deadline and scheduling each step of every project. But it's likely that her right-brained partners would prefer working in a different manner and environment. They would talk back and forth as they work, would tend to finish up their projects at the last minute, and would change things in midstream. And since they would be jumping from one project to another throughout the day, their desks would be cluttered with stacks of materials and equipment.

But a right-brained employee can feel equally uncomfortable when working in a highly structured, sterile-feeling environment. And since most of the American work world reflects a left-brained orientation, right-brained people are more often the ones being forced to function out of sync with their brain dominance. Forcing someone with a strong right-brain dominance to adhere to rules, day in and day out, could create a very unproductive scenario. Yet management principles frequently can be restructured for right-brained people—as you will discover later. In fact, if they are adapted to a right-brained working style, they can energize and enhance the right brain by adding support, organization, and balance.

Conflict can arise at work if we are paired on a project with people having an opposite dominance from ours. Left-brain-dominant people will probably want to set a detailed schedule in advance and stick with it. But the right-brained folks appear to keep wandering off in all directions with no apparent focus—much to the dismay and consternation of their left-brained counterparts. Then in a breakneck fit of speed, the right-brained workers will make the final deadline by the skin of their teeth.

As you may have already witnessed in your own job, these disparate work styles can sabotage each other and be the cause of tremendous friction and ill will. But if all team members have an understanding of the strengths of both brain dominances, a team composed of both types of workers who support each others' needs can be the best possible match. Where one style is weak and less motivated toward a particular task, the other style may be strong and well suited for it.

Brain Dominance, Personality, and Relationships

The effect of brain dominance can be felt in relationships both in and out of work. When choosing a mate, for instance, most of us are drawn toward someone of the opposite brain dominance. Then we make the mistake of assuming that what works well for us should work equally well for our partner. And nothing could be farther from the truth.

Remember, what energizes one hemisphere (and one brain dominance) tends to tire and frustrate the opposite one. Can you understand what happens in our relationships when we make the mistake of trying to force our partner to use our own system of thinking and doing things?

ACTION ITEM

Discuss with your spouse, children, or a close friend the effects of relating to someone with an opposite brain dominance. Do these different dominances get in the way of understanding and appreciating each other? In what ways can you pool your individual strengths and work preferences to create a more harmonious living and working environment?

In the realm of parenting, we adults almost always parent from our left hemispheres, enforcing rules, setting limits, and voicing expectations. Yet most children function primarily from their right hemispheres—creating clutter everywhere, breaking rules, and resisting structure—until they are in their late teens and early twenties. Can you see the possibilities for clashes and misunderstandings? Remember, both brain styles can get to the same end, but each will take an almost opposite route to do so. This leads to some interesting insights that can have a major influence not only on your energy, but also on your ability to be an effective parent and partner.

CHAPTER

"HALF-BRAINED"

DUALITY

VERSUS

WHOLE-BRAINED

INTEGRATION:

Resolving Your Mental Civil War

> ❝What it comes down to is that modern society discriminates against the right hemisphere. ❞
> —**Roger W. Sperry, Nobel Prize–winner for research on hemisphericity**

magine that you are a specta-
tor at a very unusual basketball game. One team runs up
and down the court with great
agility and speed, dodging and
leaving the other team behind.
The second team is much
slower, providing no com-
petition for the first team. As you look more closely, you
notice that each player on the second team is playing primarily on one leg, only occasionally allowing the other foot to
touch the floor. As you can imagine, the first team has more
than a double advantage over the second, for hopping on only
one foot allows much less potential and is far more tiring than
running and dodging on both feet.

This metaphor can help us understand how most of us
overlook the unlimited potential of brain integration. Even
though we all have two hemispheres and we all draw from
both throughout the day, most of us spend a large part of our
time drawing from our favorite or most skilled hemisphere
and only calling on the other here and there. An even bigger
loss is to play the mental game of trying to decide which
hemisphere is better and pitting one brain against the other. If
we stick with the basketball metaphor, it would be like having
all the players decide that it is more important and rewarding
to play offense only, so each of them would stop playing defense and would only wait for opportunities to make points.

You can imagine that without any of them playing defense, there would be no one down court to stop the other team from scoring and to bring the ball back up court. Now there might be lots of angry blaming and finger-pointing as to who should be playing defense. This often happens if one player becomes a "hot dog" and, instead of working with the other team members, just looks for every opportunity to score. Soon the other players resent this grandstanding and taking praise at their expense, and they become less and less willing to pass the ball to this player.

This is a powerful example of duality, which is breaking something into two distinct parts and then struggling over which has value or is more important. In this process, respect and trust are lost and replaced by discounting and mistrust. The very partners who have the potential to create an effective, powerful, and synergistic team use their energy and resources to defeat and thwart each other.

Now let's apply this metaphor to understand how we might use our two brain hemispheres.

Recognizing Duality

Duality occurs when each hemisphere of the brain distrusts and discounts the other. Duality is so much a part of our lives and is so ingrained in our institutions that it will be difficult to see at first. It's like pulling a big heavy door open with one hand while holding it closed with the other. Lots of energy is spent with little gain!

An example of duality might be a person who is very creative and loves to generate ideas. Being a right-brained, highly visual person, her desk is stacked with work in progress, data from phone calls, and files with research information. If she rarely devotes time and energy to filing away work and resists allowing others to file work, she soon becomes buried in the prolific generation of good ideas and can have a breakdown following up on them. I know this painfully from my own patterns of duality. My right brain becomes like a rebellious kid as I "creatively" stay too busy to attend to the chores I don't enjoy. Meanwhile my left brain becomes very judgmental, nagging me for the "awful mess" I work in and creating great internal anxiety as I imagine all the terrible things that might result from my out-of-balance and out-of-control state.

If you are smugly thinking you would never fall into such a state of disorganization, consider the duality from the left brain. Here a person rarely if ever risks trying something totally new. He insists on the comfort of staying close to the "standard" way of doing things and demands perfection even when he knows it is no longer working. He is big on accuracy and the tried-and-true ways of doing things, insisting: "If it ain't broke, don't fix it." When presented with ideas for innovative improvements, he may quickly find fault and resist. His strengths are in details and order. Although his desk will be clean, his mind may be resistant or closed to innovation or new ways to solve old problems.

The following, from *The Experts Speak: The Definitive Compendium of Authoritative Misinformation,* by Christopher Cerf and Victor Navasky, are classic examples of duality where the so-called experts were the most resistant to change and blind to new ways of thinking:

"Everything that can be invented has been invented."
(Charles H. Duell, commissioner of the U.S. Office of Patents, urging President William McKinley to abolish his office in 1899)

"When the Paris Exhibition closes, electric light will close with it and no more will be heard of it."
(Erasmus Wilson, professor at Oxford University, 1878)

"I think there is a world market for about five computers."
(attributed to Thomas J. Watson, Sr., chairman of the board of International Business Machines, 1943)

Recognizing Duality in Yourself and Others

If you think of duality as one side of your brain wanting one thing while the other side pushes for the opposite result, you have a good picture of what is taking place. For example, when you awaken to your alarm clock, one side of your brain expects you to get up promptly and begin getting dressed for your day. The other side of your brain may wish to stay snuggled warmly under the covers, peacefully dozing for just a bit longer. Next you may feel guilt and judgment coming from your impatient left brain while the rebellious right brain invents a reason to stay snug for just a bit longer. It becomes hard to enjoy those last few minutes with the left brain nagging and blaming, reminding you of all the other times you wasted precious minutes sleeping your life away when you could have been getting that all-important early start!

Can you remember any mornings like this? When we slip into duality, we experience a mental civil war, with each hemisphere out to punish and sabotage the other as an adversary rather than wanting to team with the other as a partner. Our language can signal duality and an opportunity to shift into brain integration. The following phrases are a tip-off to duality:

"I've got to . . ."	or	"You've got to . . ."
"I have to . . ."	or	"You have to . . ."
"I must . . ."	or	"You must . . ."
"I should . . ."	or	"You should . . ."

The issue is *control.* You feel pressured by yourself or whoever is saying you must or should do something. There is no trust that you will follow through without coaxing or nagging. You can think of this as the left brain pressuring and attempting to control the right brain. Notice that in response, your right brain typically becomes resistant and defensive. You might find yourself thinking of why you don't want to do whatever you "should" do. You may behave much like a rebellious child, thinking of ways to put off or resist the pressure to perform.

In these examples you can see the two aspects of duality: the discounting and the distrust of each hemisphere for the other met with resistance, defensive blocked thinking, and often rebellion. Can you see why this mental tug of war drains so much energy? One part of you is literally nagging and cajoling, much as a bossy parent might, while the other part of you becomes the rebellious child, resenting advice and instruction even if it is in your best interest.

Choosing Brain Integration over Duality

To shift yourself out of duality, think of these two parts of yourself working as a cooperative team. If you decided with your logical left brain to get up early and get on the road ahead of the traffic, your left brain might gently remind your right brain of how good it will feel to miss the traffic and get to the office early. Remember that the right brain responds much as a kid might, so think of reasoning with a child. Rewarding the child in you with something appealing may be a successful strategy. As you lie in bed, visualize your day, imaging how well you will perform and how much you will be respected by being early and well prepared. Then plan something special as a reward, such as listening to a tape you enjoy while on the toll road or meeting your spouse at a special restaurant for dinner. These images invite your right brain to join the left in choosing wholeheartedly to get up early.

This choice clearly indicates brain integration. When all of you chooses to do something, both of your hemispheres cooperate and are in agreement. When you feel as if part of you wants to do something and part doesn't, you are in duality. And it is this push/pull argument between the two parts that erodes your precious energy. Thus, integration is *drawing on the benefits of both sides of the brain.* There is high trust, cooperation, and appreciation between and for both hemispheres.

The Language of Integration

A quick way to shift yourself into brain integration is simply to use such phrases as these:

"I choose to . . . "

"I get to . . . "

"I look forward to . . . "

"I want to . . . "

These indicate that your logical left brain and your emotional right brain are together on each decision. As a result, your logic joins your enthusiasm in entering into these commitments. The problem with "have to's" is that they make us feel controlled, and we have a natural tendency to resist control. This resistance we set up for ourselves drains our personal energy. Can you feel the difference, as you think of real choices in your life, in shifting from "have to" to "choose to"?

For example, let's consider paying income taxes. You may think of that as a "have to" job and feel you have no choice in the matter. Certainly nobody wants to pay taxes. Let's test this assumption.

"If you don't want to pay your taxes, then don't."

"But if I don't, I will go to jail."

"Then go to jail."

"But I don't want to go to jail."

"Then it sounds like you may want to pay your taxes."

You may not like your choices, but you do have a choice. Of even greater importance is the freedom to choose your attitude and the energy drain or gain that goes with it. Since you get more energy by changing a "have to" task to a "choose to" or "want to" task, you can take this idea a step further and add more energy by saying, "I get to pay my taxes." You may discover not only new energy but new reasons why there really is a "get to" in the situation. For example, with taxes we get to live in a free country and to help fund well-built highways, hospitals, parks, and social programs. We can easily find as many reasons to feel good about "getting" to pay our share of the taxes as we previously found for feeling bad about "having" to pay them. It's all a matter of discovering a new perspective—and integrated thinking.

Duality: Splitting Our Brain into the Rebellious Child Versus the Merciless Master

We have named the personalities of our two hemispheres the Rebellious Child (right brain) and the Merciless Master (left brain). When you are in duality, your right hemisphere behaves much like a rebellious child, sulking, feeling guilty, and being a victim with no options but to blame others and wallow in self-pity. In this "poor me" mood, a person is hard to deal

Duality Self-Talk

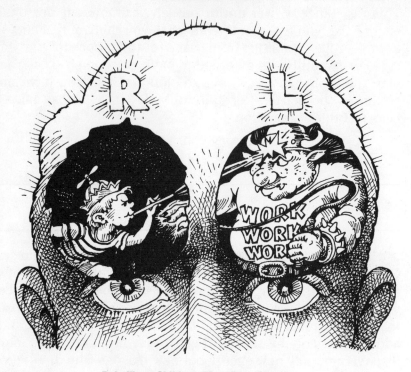

Rebellious Child vs. Merciless Master

with. This is the defensive self, full of excuses and unwilling to be held accountable for any actions. Attempts to get the person to be more objective and solution-oriented will be seen as unsupportive attacks.

The left hemisphere is the Merciless Master. When you are in a state of duality, this part is never satisfied with your performance, is constantly critical, and demands more and more. The Merciless Master fears play and celebrations as a threat and condemns such behavior as wasting time and being complacent instead of constantly forging ahead. When the Rebellious Child becomes more active, the Merciless Master becomes more aggressive, feeling justified in lowering the boom. This becomes a self-perpetuating, negative spiral, endlessly draining energy and self-image.

You can also project these two parts of the personality

Integration Self-Talk

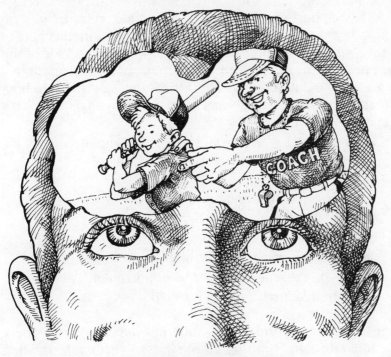

Free Child and Supportive Coach

onto other people. When you are in duality, you perceive others to be in duality as well. They are good or bad, black or white. You fear playfulness in others because you can't control your own playfulness (in the form of your Rebellious Child).

Brain Integration:
Teaming the Free Child with the Supportive Coach

Now let's look at how these two hemispheres can become transformed into two cooperative, interdependent partners. We call them the Free Child (right brain) and the Supportive Coach (left brain). Notice how the same parts of us that were operating like a Rebellious Child and a Merciless Master can become positive. As the Free Child, our right brain becomes eager, playful, cooperative, enthusiastic, and creative in response to our Supportive Coach, who nurtures, guides, protects, and encourages the positive growth of the Free Child.

The Supportive Coach is the analytical, measuring, strategic side of the brain. But in a state of integration, this part of us totally supports and values all the opposite qualities of the right brain. It knows that curiosity, innovation, and spontaneity are essential for creative breakthroughs, so it helps in honing and evaluating, but always from a positive position. This part of your brain

- knows when to nurture and when to discipline;
- encourages dreams of excellence as well as outrageous dreams;
- provides structure and discipline;
- is firm but fair;
- uses positive affirmations;
- helps you move past fears and learn from mistakes;
- helps you reframe problems as opportunities; and
- can admit failures and ask for help.

There is high trust and cooperation between these two opposite but mutually supportive partners, with each drawing energy and insight from the other.

A clear example of the effectiveness of brain integration is my own experience of working on a typewriter versus a word processor. I once worked for a bank president who insisted that everything be typed perfectly the first time. No erasures or corrections were allowed! (Can you hear the Merciless Master in this?) As I would get to the bottom of a complex page of typing, I would become more and more tense, fearing that one small error would cause me to have to begin again. And, like a self-fulfilling prophecy, this frequently happened.

Working on a word processor now, I notice that both my typing speed and my accuracy have increased tremendously, primarily because any error can be corrected easily with no fear of punishment or embarrassment. The word processor is like a Supportive Coach, giving me ways to make my work better and even coaching me through its spell checker. I look forward to and get energy from writing on a word processor,

ACTION ITEM

One way to avoid the victim mentality is to "harvest" problems. Focus on seeking solutions rather than on laying blame. Invite both hemispheres to help each other without blaming by asking, "What can I learn from this problem that will help me in the future?" or "If I had it to do over again, what could I do differently?"

whereas I used to experience writer's block and dreaded "having" to write on a typewriter.

Here is an analogy that may help you understand how we can try to integrate the divergent elements within ourselves. Imagine that you are boarding an airplane and find yourself seated next to a man and a three-year-old child. The child is whining, pouring orange juice into your seat, suffering from a runny nose, and about to burst into a full-blown tantrum. Meanwhile, the father is casually flipping through a magazine and pretending the child does not exist. The flight lasts for five hours. How do you feel about taking your seat? Now imagine instead that you are taking the same seat, but the father and the three-year-old are happily and quietly playing a game together. The child looks up at you with sparkling eyes and greets you with a big joyous grin. Would you feel differently about spending five hours with this child?

In fact, all of us have that child within us all the time. We can either ignore it, make it feel that the only way it can get our attention is by behaving obnoxiously, and try to beat it down, or we can nurture it, give it opportunities to play, and support it in dealing with fears and anxieties. Obviously, the child who is nurtured is the Free Child, who brings us joy.

Self-Directed or Proactive Versus the Victim Mentality

One final tip for catching yourself when you have slipped into duality is to observe your level of motivation. When you are in duality, you will feel as though you are having to force yourself to do things. You may drag yourself to the office and then sit there limply, without the enthusiasm or motivation to plunge into the day. This is classic duality. It also describes burnout, which results from living in duality. In this mental state we operate out of the victim mentality, not seeing the many opportunities to make our lives positive and satisfying but instead blaming others for our dissatisfaction and lack of success:

"My boss doesn't . . ."

"My parents didn't . . ."

"When I was in college, they didn't teach me . . ."

There are endless excuses and ways to blame others. But when we blame ourselves, we don't take action or persevere. When you feel yourself being dragged down by this mental struggle, be gentle with yourself. Start by nurturing those two battered parts of your thinking, and then gently bring each part into a mutually supportive team. You will then unite these two parts as working, cooperative partners within yourself. When you do this, you are self-directed rather than dependent on others to "make" you do whatever needs to be done. This cooperation is proactive rather than reactive. It means planning ahead and deciding in advance what you want as a total picture of your day and week instead of reactively taking one thing at a time.

One business is encouraging integration in both employees and youngsters through a new program. Principal Financial Group, a Des Moines insurance company, gives prizes to elementary school kids for good health and study habits. This program doesn't just recognize A's on report cards. Instead, kids get rewarded for brushing their teeth, playing baseball, reading books, and doing both right- and left-brain activities. The hoped-for result will be early habits that promote integration and discourage duality.

When you invite your two hemispheres to become partners in living your life, you will reap the benefits of long-term planning (which will keep you from suffering from last-minute crises) as well as the joy of living in the moment, being totally present to each event and person in your life. There is a wonderful synergy that comes from this union.

Duality Attitudes (Half-Brained)

1. Play is frivolous (left brain).
2. I keep playfulness out of the office (left brain).
3. I and others have to be frightened, coerced, or forced into work (left brain).
4. Anything I want to do at any time is okay regardless of the rights of others (right brain).
5. I put things off to create a crisis because I do my best work under pressure (right brain).
6. If I stop to play, I can't trust myself or others to get back to work (left brain).

Duality Behaviors

1. I see every situation as win-lose, a battle or competition to be won.

2. I see life only in absolutes—black or white, my way vs. your way.
3. I am dependent and/or independent, unwilling to delegate or delegating only with elaborate, resistive instructions.

Integration Attitudes (Whole-Brained)

1. Playfulness can enhance my work.
2. I enjoy breaks *and* the opportunity to work.
3. I and others work better when motivated through positive support, trust, and challenge.
4. I value my freedom but value equally the rights and freedom of others.
5. I replace last-minute crises with planning for challenges in advance.
6. Trust and intrinsic motivation are the foundation for personal and team productivity.

Integration Behaviors

1. I see every situation as an opportunity for teaming; I want things to work out as well for others as for myself; I don't demand credit or the spotlight; I emphasize cooperation, creating synergy.
2. I realize there is more than one right answer.
3. I am interdependent, not only delegating the job, but also trusting the other person to decide how to get it done.

ACTION ITEM

How do you know if you are becoming more whole-brained? This is a beginning list to help those interested in brain transformation to continue personal growth. As you read down the list, you might look for opportunities to expand your frame of reference and appreciation. After reading each question, rate your current behavior patterns on the scale ("1" means seldom or not a part of your behavior; "10" means consistently a part of your behavior).

1. I am open to and interested in ways of thinking that are unlike my own. When others differ with me, I am curious and open to learning a new way of seeing and thinking rather than assuming that they are wrong or that one of us has to be wrong.

1   2   3   4   5   6   7   8   9   10

2. I am learning to be equally interested in strongly left-brained ways of thinking and working as well as strongly right-brained ways.

1   2   3   4   5   6   7   8   9   10

3. When my spouse or children disagree or differ with me, I am able to listen to and learn from their point of view. I am learning from others that having one right answer to everything is too narrow.

1   2   3   4   5   6   7   8   9   10

4. I am learning to have fun doing things that I used to think were silly or not my cup of tea. I purposely seek out these new experiences to broaden my perspective.

1   2   3   4   5   6   7   8   9   10

5. I seek ways to play that are not competitive. I am able to enjoy being curious and full of wonder rather than having to compete or win to be entertained. (Or, if your fun is typically noncompetitive, you might seek out more competitive fun as a means to balance. You will be the best judge of your needs and balance point.)

1   2   3   4   5   6   7   8   9   10

6. My work is fun, satisfying, and fulfilling to me. I am able to enjoy even parts of my work that could be considered routine or drudgery in the fuller context of my mission. I am also very creative in finding ways to enjoy the unenjoyable.

1   2   3   4   5   6   7   8   9   10

7.   I have an equal dedication to my play and to my work. I take time to refresh myself and relax regularly, so I can work with more creativity and energy.

1   2   3   4   5   6   7   8   9   10

8.   I am able to admit my mistakes openly and learn from them with little or no self-punishment or guilt. I talk about my mistakes openly to encourage others to feel equally comfortable about their mistakes. I see them as opportunities to learn and necessary steps toward innovation and growth.

1   2   3   4   5   6   7   8   9   10

9.   I take good care of myself—my body as well as my mental and spiritual self. I enjoy eating healthy food most of the time and enjoy healthy aerobic exercise on a regular basis.

1   2   3   4   5   6   7   8   9   10

10.   I typically choose to view problems as opportunities. I spend very little time overwhelmed and discouraged. I am aware of a wide range of resources personally, socially, and professionally. I am convinced that creative people look for innovative new ways to view the situation and make breakthroughs where others choose to be stumped by the "impossible." I enjoy brainstorming new ideas as well as following through on the details to project completion.

1   2   3   4   5   6   7   8   9   10

11.   I am consistent with my attitudes and behaviors; my team and family know they can come to me any time about anything and I will be open and supportive.

1   2   3   4   5   6   7   8   9   10

12.   I stay in touch with my feelings and am comfortable expressing anger, grief, joy, love, and other emotions. I can give clear messages without blaming or accusing.

1   2   3   4   5   6   7   8   9   10

13.   I recognize the principle: "In order to keep, I must give away." As I come into more balance and brain integration, I value sharing with others (e.g., role modeling, teaching, listening) *for my benefit*.

1   2   3   4   5   6   7   8   9   10

Note: If you found yourself frustrated and confused by being asked to arbitrarily rate yourself with no clear, measurable criteria, be aware that this indicates your strengths in left-brained processing. Realize that to become truly whole-brained, *intangibles* must become as obvious, measured, and valued as *tangibles*. To grow toward whole-brain synthesis, you may want to risk making some "guesstimates" or inviting others who know you well to give you feedback. Or you may want to just skip over the rating scale, but reflect on where and how you can grow.

BURNOUT
SYMPTOMS:
Avoiding Traps That Drain Your Energy

How do we know when we are in duality? Typically it results in burnout, so let's examine the symptoms and see what we can learn:

> *I wake up tired, I go to sleep tired, I just don't seem to have the energy to do much of anything anymore.*

> *Even a vacation sounds like too much of an effort to be worth it. Nothing I can think of sounds like fun to me.*

> *I have an overwhelming case of the I-don't-want-tos.*

> *I feel a lot like I'm on a treadmill, going nowhere fast.*

All of these comments on the preceding page are the familiar symptoms of burnout. You can get a minor case after a few weeks of pushing too hard without relief, or you can fall into a major case of burnout after a few years of living out of balance. Like the flu, it can be a temporary setback that leaves you drained and out of sorts, or it can lead to major depression. Like the flu, burnout is something to which you are never immune!

The symptoms are all basically "lack of" symptoms, lack of

- energy,
- enthusiasm,
- motivation,
- ideas,
- permission to play,
- humor,

- joy,
- satisfaction,
- interest,
- dreams for life,
- concentration, or
- self-confidence.

There are at least three symptoms of burnout that can be called dysfunctional:

1. **Sexuality.** You may lose interest in sex or find yourself unfulfilled no matter how much you experience.
2. **Appetite.** You may lose your interest in eating or want to eat everything in sight—primarily junk food. Again, you seem to be eating without feeling fulfilled.

3. **Sleep.** You may not be able to sleep or you may over-sleep, using sleep as an escape from a life that has lost its interest. You awaken tired and listless.

The list goes on. We each have our own personal symptoms:

- feeling grouchy or irritable or endlessly tired;
- being unwilling and unable to be pleased;
- wanting something but not being sure what it is;
- dwelling on the negatives in life and within ourselves;
- feeling that it will be too much trouble and take too much energy to enjoy pastimes that used to be fun;
- feeling hopelessly trapped on a treadmill;
- becoming a cross bearer;
- seeing too many things to do and too little time to do them.

Or you can be in the "I don't wanna" syndrome: "I don't wanna go to work," "I can't think of anything that sounds like fun," "I don't wanna do my chores or see friends."

Victim mentality is a classic symptom of burnout. Typically we are blind to how we trap ourselves into this role and then believe it is others who are holding us as their victim. We may feel that we have to work long hours or even hold two jobs to pay for our house, to keep our kids in college, to pay our bills. Or we may feel trapped by our boss who expects us to work evenings and weekends. Whatever our trap, we end up feeling that everyone we know but us has a life. We don't have time to exercise, to eat healthy food, to enjoy our families, to participate in social events or hobbies. We end up blaming the job, the kids, the boss, or our spouse for making our life more miserable—even though our choices have led us to this point.

When we slip into the victim mentality, the next step is *denial.* Technically, we are in denial when we are unable to acknowledge the link between our choices and our dilemma. Even if others show us possible options, we can't admit that they exist. Here is one example:

A mother chooses to do everything for her kids—she cooks, cleans up after them, does their laundry, keeps the house, and drives them wherever they want to go. As a result they never learn to help with chores or assume responsibility for themselves. When they become teenagers, they get credit cards. Can you see what happens next? The mother, a victim in her own mind, wrings her hands about the spiraling bills, the irresponsible behavior of her children, and her own pitiful condition, but she can't see the obvious (to everyone else) answer to the problem: take away the cards and insist that her teenagers take responsibility for earning the money they want.

Denial will sabotage effective teamwork—within the home or at work. Burnout keeps people from facing a situation squarely, looking for creative solutions, and working together to solve problems. It becomes a giant obstacle to all the major goals of any successful business or family situation. Furthermore, burnout is extremely contagious and can spread from one member of the group to the next with incredible rapidity!

A second side effect of burnout is *unhealthy control.* When we refuse to take charge of our own behavior, we become exhausted and lose our patience; we then blow up or feel justified in setting punitive limits on others. A healthy alternative would be open dialogue, in which we ask for what we want and need in advance, limiting our role of overparenting or overmanaging others.

A vital key is to realize that burnout is not something that happens only once in a lifetime. It can creep into our lives again and again. If we learn to recognize our symptoms, we can catch it before great damage has been done and regain our balance quickly.

These symptoms all have in common the dimension of being out of balance. In fact, *burnout is the result of living out of balance.* Often, there is a short-term reward for doing so. For example, there is some big project at work, you are starting your own business, or you are going back to graduate school while raising a family or holding down a job—any of these can demand a superhuman effort. In the short term you are willing to pay the price. Then one day you find yourself in burnout without the energy to cope. In this condition, denial sets in and you may not have the energy to see solutions. You become your own worst enemy.

In the short term the solution may seem to be to live out of balance and push for the immediate goal. However, you may reach your immediate goal only to lose something of greater worth, such as your physical or mental health, a marriage, or unreclaimable time with your children.

Ellen Terry, mother of two children and president and owner of Ellen Terry Realtors, shares her experience:

"Real estate is a unique profession where many of your clients will expect you to be on call twenty-four hours a day, seven days a week. When I started in real estate, I realized I was becoming a workaholic and that I would burn out soon if I kept up at the pace I was going. It's easy to become addicted to the excitement and high pressure, but once I stepped back from my frenzied schedule, I saw that I needed to have more time for myself, and that I could have rewarding, fun times away from work. In the past I defined myself only as a businesswoman and a mother. I spent too much time focusing on being a 'human-doing,' not a 'human-being.' If I wasn't climbing a mountain businesswise, I wasn't a worthwhile person. But now I am trying to live more in the present moment."

In the next chapters, we will look at three profiles that lead to burnout—perfectionism, "fast-lane" living, and the superhuman syndrome. Each is linked to high performance in some way and is easy to slip into because most corporations and many families reward and encourage these behaviors. In the short term each can bring high performance, but in the long term they are burnout traps. See what you can learn about yourself as we examine them.

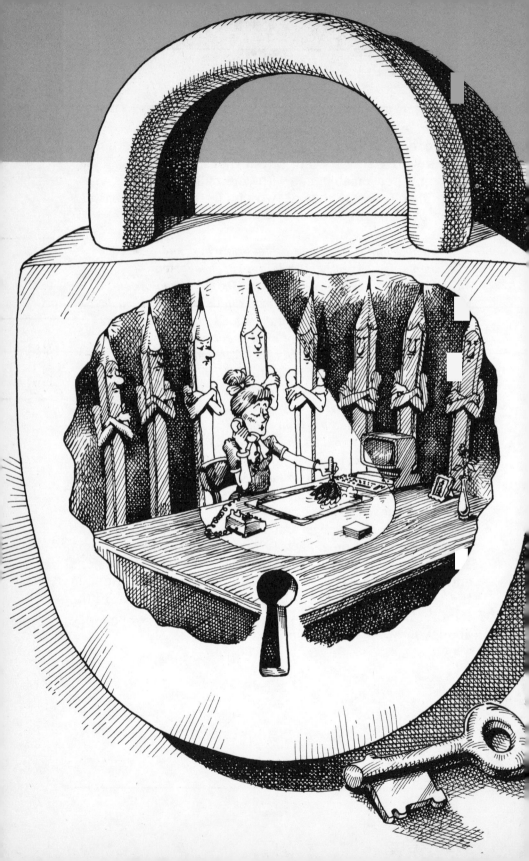

THE PERILS OF PERFECTIONISM:

When the Juice Ain't Worth the Squeeze

" *Compulsive perfectionism polishes the past when bold new skills are needed to unlock the future.* **"**
—**Dag Hammarskjöld**

" *Success is going from failure to failure without loss of enthusiasm.* **"**
—**Winston Churchill**

" *He who deliberates fully before taking a step will spend his entire life on one leg.* **"**
—**Chinese proverb**

" *Aim for success, not perfection. Never give up your right to be wrong, because then you will lose the ability to learn new things and move forward with your life.* **"**
—**Dr. David M. Burns**

ranted, much satisfaction can be gained by doing a job exceptionally well and by meeting your personal expectations, whether by completing a project under budget or giving a flawless speech. But do you devote the same painstaking time and effort to nearly everything you do? Do you perform each task as meticulously as the next? Are your hedges always neatly trimmed, your furniture polished, your interoffice memos formally composed and typed, all pieces of correspondence promptly answered?

People who have taken the dictate "Anything worth doing is worth doing well" too seriously are unwilling or unable to discriminate between important and unimportant tasks and areas in their lives. Yet many of us believe in this ideal because we had it pounded into our heads by some very influential people, such as parents, teachers, coaches, or dancing and music instructors. However, this maxim becomes impractical and even unproductive when we grow up and lead extremely busy, complex lives.

Perfectionism is a fairly common personality profile in the business world. The Action Item can help you decide whether this personality profile fits you and, if so, to what extent.

ACTION ITEM

Put a check mark next to the statements that describe you.

☐ I get upset with myself whenever I don't do something well, even if I'm a novice at it.

☐ I suffer through a game of golf or tennis (intended as fun and relief from work) when I'm not playing at my best.

☐ I shy away from trying new things.

☐ I often lose patience with my colleagues or my children if they don't catch on to something quickly.

☐ I rarely think of shortcuts for doing everyday projects, such as home maintenance, chores, meal preparation, correspondence, or running errands.

☐ I have a reputation at work of being someone who is hard to please.

☐ I usually refuse to start a project unless I have all the optimum equipment or ingredients for it (for example, I may refuse to prepare a certain meal because I am out of one of the spices called for in the recipe or I may refuse to let my secretary send out a routine letter because one small, unimportant piece of information is still missing).

If you answer yes to most of the Action Item questions, it is safe to conclude that you have bought into this energy-wasting pattern of behavior. Sometimes it is difficult to recognize these tendencies in ourselves, so you should consider getting your spouse's or friends' judgments about any perfectionist tendencies you might have.

Of course, it is admirable and important to perform well in the significant areas of your life. And most successful people hope to perform exceptionally well—in fact, best—at some of their endeavors. The problem, and energy waste, arises when they can't prioritize the relative value of each task (because all tasks must be done equally meticulously); can't accept less-than-perfect performance on some tasks (because they can't ever see themselves as doing something with less than their best effort); can't accept imperfection in others (because they can't conceive of value systems other than their own); and are unwilling to attempt something new that they might not excel at (because they can't tolerate the idea of being mediocre at anything).

Perfectionism

The *Lure*   is to be perfect, having a reputation of always being right and reliable and exceptional.

The *Payoff*   is to be completely in control, earning people's attention and awe, and knowing that you always meet your highest expectations of yourself.

The *Trap*   is that your identity becomes fused with perfectionism. Down deep you know you aren't perfect at everything, but you can't admit this lack of perfection. You work harder and harder to maintain the impossible role of being perfect at everything and get less and less satisfaction from your effort. You fear change, experimentation, and adventure because they might result in less than perfect results and therefore you give up the very things that are key sources of renewed energy. Another version of this is to confuse perfection with excellence and quality. When we do this, we ignore the law of diminishing returns. In business, if we can't prioritize time spent on tasks, we lose money.

Recall a day when you did everything perfectly. Perhaps you gave a tried-and-true speech of yours to a community group, then repeated a reliable sales-pitch formula to a new client, and took another potential client out to lunch at your favorite restaurant. Later you stayed two hours overtime at the office to triple-check a report of yours, even though two people had already proofed it. Mentally recall the specifics of your own perfect day.

Whatever it was like, we can assure you that if you did everything perfectly, you were not growing but were merely standing still, repeating what you had already perfected. On the other hand, on the days when you allow yourself to attempt new skills and to grow, you are bound to make some mistakes. You are also bound to feel unsure and inexperienced at first and to do some things clumsily. But this is a necessary stage to work through if you wish to learn something new and grow as a person.

Unfortunately, many perfection-minded adults rarely risk learning a new sport or game because they become so dependent upon the image of themselves as being right and capable that they feel uncomfortable whenever they return to the role of a rank beginner. Thus they are destined to stay in one place for the rest of their lives, only polishing (perfecting) what they already know. Usually these folks live at less than peak energy. First, they deny themselves the energy-producing experiences of facing totally new situations, processing fresh information, feeling satisfaction at learning a new skill, and even experiencing some apprehension. These experiences, by the way, are key stimulants in the child's world of play. Second, they expend too much energy worrying about doing everything meticulously. By trying to do everything equally perfectly rather than doing some things very well and less important things only satisfactorily, they often squander their time and energy rather than preserving it for their most important responsibilities and goals. Finally, even when they do participate in activities that should be relaxing and fun, such as playing bridge or tennis with friends or jogging by themselves, they place such high standards on themselves to perform admirably that these activities become competitive trials filled with pressure. That can take all the fun out of them and turn a potential energy gain into an energy drain. Thus most perfectionists end up expending more energy than they regain, an energy loss cycle that ultimately leads to burnout.

If you fall into this category, ask yourself, What does it take to be perfect? In fact, perfectionism requires so much time that you may be much less productive and ingenious than those who are less perfect. Perfectionists are forever seeing a tiny flaw to correct. This consuming attention to every detail, which they feel no one else can handle, takes time. Perfectionists tend to produce less, take fewer chances, stick to procedure rather than create new solutions, and be overprotective about their own territory. Rather than being well-rounded, they tend to be narrow and short-sighted. In contrast, our research into the lives of people considered to be geniuses finds them leading very diverse lives filled with many interests, some they are masters at and some they just find enjoyable. But this diversity is one of the primary sources for their discoveries. Their many interests give them a large basis of knowledge and a constant source of stimulation for new creative links and insights.

Research has shown that most major breakthroughs come from accidental discoveries, often by amateurs who are experimenting purely from the love of the subject. The word *amateur* comes from the Latin *amare* or "to love." People who love their work, love their play, and love their hobbies are more likely to find new insights and come up with totally new ways of doing things than those who are immersed in the old paradigm. We now know that love, joy, and passion trigger endorphins, the chemical reactions in the brain that lead to even more creativity and innovation.

If you need another argument against compulsive, perfectionist behavior, consider how much extra time it takes to do everything equally well rather than doing low-priority items just adequately. Take, for example, the task of altering a skirt. A quick tuck in the waistband is a five-minute job, a makeshift alteration that will never show under a jacket. The "proper" way to alter the skirt would be to remove the waistband, shorten it, reset the button or hooks, and then restitch the band in place. Why do it except to be perfect? Only you and the dry cleaner know which you do! (An even faster solution can be achieved with a big safety pin!)

When you catch yourself behaving like a perfectionist, realize that you are experiencing one of the early symptoms of burnout and that there are ways to stop this negative energy spiral. Here are some of our techniques for minimizing this behavior pattern.

Addictions

Addictions are behaviors that mask our pain, stress, and feelings of low self-esteem. When we feel overwhelmed, out of control, and hopelessly behind on everything, our addictions kick in. Perfectionism is one addiction, but there are many more. We begin by enjoying whatever we do with excellence. We are satisfied to see perfect work and to hear the approval of others, but soon we are addicted to perfection. Our identity gets confused and fused with excellent performance and we are afraid not to push as far as possible with everything we do. Suddenly, we have created a trap for ourselves. We can't enjoy the effort anymore because we know it isn't quite perfect enough and we feel a need to do even more.

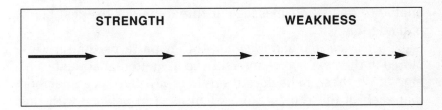

Think of any personal strength or gift as being on a continuum. When we are under pressure, we put more and more energy into our strength. At some point it turns into a weakness. You know you have gone from a strength (choosing to bring excellence to your work) to a weakness (becoming obsessed by perfectionism) when you feel compelled to do everything perfectly instead of choosing how much effort to put into each task.

Perfectionism is just one addiction. Overeating or eating too much salt, sugar, fat, or caffeine can be addictions. The more we eat, the less we taste and the more we crave. When we feel discouraged, worthless, or behind in our work, we are apt to head for our addictions.

We can also become addicted to other behavior patterns, including:

Workaholism—getting satisfaction from working longer and longer hours and covering negative feelings by burying ourselves in work. The problem is that we stop thinking creatively and end up pushing blindly toward an unsatisfying finish.

Control—feeling valuable by bossing others. If our feelings of self-worth come from controlling others, we are in a constantly unrewarding position. The more we boss others, the more we create resistance and resentment in them. By teaching them to depend on us so that they'll do what they don't want to do, we create "learned helplessness." Now we hear, "You didn't wake me up in time" or "Why didn't you tell me I needed gas in the car?" We create a role for ourselves and feel very important because everyone around us seems to need us. Yet this is unhealthy for everyone. In reality, we are interfering with others' best performance and not contributing productively ourselves. If anyone tries to point this out to us, watch out! We will probably be in denial and unable to hear their message. It threatens our deepest fears of inadequacy.

Fast track and superhuman—other patterns that are explored in the next two chapters. Keep in mind that at the beginning of all these behaviors there is a payoff. Also remember that each of these behaviors, when used in balance with the needs and talents of others, can be healthy and positive. It is only when one thing becomes supremely important—food, control, perfectionism—that it becomes a problem.

Look for signals that you are becoming trapped. You may feel out of balance, like a victim. When we feel cut off from the help and teaming of others because we think that only we can do what we are doing, we need to stop and take a good look. That is the red-light signal of addiction flashing its warning at you.

Cures for Perfectionism

Cure 1: Harvest the good, or apply the 96 percent versus 4 percent assessment rule. When you were a kid in the second grade and you got a 96 on a spelling or math exam, how did you feel? Were you satisfied with the A, or did you browbeat yourself about the four points you missed?

As an adult, how often do you commute home at the end of a hard day, focusing only on the 4 percent of your efforts that you didn't do well? Do you often berate yourself for making a mistake, then fabricate worst-case scenarios for all the horrible consequences that might befall you? The more you dwell on those few errors, the more magnified they become. By the time you reach home, that 4 percent feels more like 40 percent, so you feel frustrated, pressured, and even embarrassed by your "poor performance" or "wasted" day.

Two well-known researchers of human behavior and longevity have reported on the importance of highlighting one's daily successes rather than one's mistakes. Jean Houston and Robert Masters interviewed a large population of highly active men and women in their seventies, eighties, and nineties, such as Pablo Casals, Margaret Mead, Fred Astaire, and Bob Hope. When asked how they had the energy and drive to keep working at their advanced ages, many of them described a phenomenon that Houston and Masters termed "harvesting." For example, a typical response would be: "In my seventies I went through something like a second adolescence. I discovered that I was worrying about all the wrong things. Then I learned how to let go of worry; it merely saps energy and enthusiasm. Instead I taught myself how to harvest. At the end of the day I would ask myself what I had learned. And if I had made some mistakes, I asked myself what insights I could harvest from them. Thus I put all my energy into learning and none into blaming myself or others, none into feeling badly about myself."

Another practical tip comes from Dave Cole, vice president of Petroleum & Petrochemical, Fluor Daniel, Inc.:

> *"Let me tell you something that has made a tremendous difference for me. The nature of my job is to spend a great deal of my time solving problems and anticipating problems—it is very easy to get into a less than positive frame of mind when this is your primary daily focus. One simple but extremely effective whole-brained suggestion is, on the way home each evening, to think only of the good things that happened that day. I've been doing this for a number of months now. It amazes me how many really great things happen during the course of a day. And the benefit is that my wife, Donna, quite clearly notices the difference when I walk in the door. The result is more evening quality time!"*

Cure 2: Put a high value on "failing forward." Failure is a loss only if you fail to learn from the experience. Again, by studying the lives of successful leaders, we have discovered that they commonly see failure not as something to be avoided at all costs but rather as an opportunity to learn and grow.

Thomas Edison, for example, once was asked how he came to hold more patents than any other person. He answered that he dared to make more mistakes than ten other people put together and had learned from each of them. Then he remarked, "And sooner or later I find a way to patent most of them." Edison knew full well that the creative process involves the technique of turning problems into opportunities and unpolished ideas into gems. So if you are someone who dares to venture into problem areas, you will in fact have more opportunities and innovative successes than most others. And people will stand in awe of you, appreciating your pioneering spirit and ingenuity.

One way that businesses are finding new options is by loosening up the traditional hierarchical structure where innovation and ideas always come from the top. General Motors attributes its rising quality to a new policy of opening up communication about quality to every level—from assembly line workers to engineers, from suppliers to designers. Don Schneider, CEO of Schneider National Trucking, found his business in chaos when the industry was deregulated. He responded by flattening and democratizing the organization. All employees are known as "associates," and status symbols like reserved parking were removed. According to Schneider, the process worked: "You deemphasize title and emphasize the ability and the importance of the person." When everyone is invited to speak his or her mind, offer creative solutions, and participate in decision making, there *is* risk involved, but there are also many new options for forward movement.

Which leads us to another strategy for breaking out of the perfectionist mold: making a list of areas, both job-related and otherwise, that you would like to explore but haven't for fear of not doing well at them. Maybe you have a hunch about an unusual way to solve some problem at work or a daring concept for publicizing a new product your company is developing. Perhaps there's a hobby or sport you'd like to take up or a different way to spend your summer vacation this year. Take time to write down your thoughts, then take a chance on these ideas. Though all of them may not pan out to your expectations, surely some will. And the others will bring fresh insights into your life and your work. The main skill to learn from this exercise, however, is how to cope with risk taking and how to stretch into new areas of your life.

Cure 3: Do one thing imperfectly each day. We are indebted to Dru Scott and her book *How to Put More Time in Your Life* for this marvelous idea. Hard-core perfectionists will find this difficult to do, yet it is an effective first step for breaking out of their mold. We suggest starting off with small things: cooking a new style of food; striking up a conversation with someone whom you don't know (and whose reactions you can't anticipate); playing a game you are not familiar with; asking your secretary to teach you about an unfamiliar machine or process; reading a book that you think might be "over your head" or contrary to your set beliefs; learning a new hobby or exercise routine. By doing this you will learn to accept your initial feelings of awkwardness and insecurity. You will actually come to enjoy the sense of challenge and satisfaction that comes from trying something new, no matter how unpolished your first attempts are. And you will learn to accept the "imperfect learner" side of you, which we hope will make you feel more willing to attempt other worthwhile but uncertain opportunities that come your way.

On a more practical note, being willing to do some things imperfectly will save you time and wasted energy. I've applied my "do one thing imperfectly each day" rule to my work routine and have discovered some valuable shortcuts. For example, the large majority of my mail can be handled quickly by simply writing a note on the bottom of the letter or by dictating an outline of my thoughts that my secretary can later "perfect" into a full response. Then I save my full energy for the 10 percent of the mail that requires my personal attention.

I have also learned to have a much less fastidious attitude toward my house. My new policy is to recruit everyone in my family to be his or her own maid. They are each responsible for cleaning up their own dirty dishes, dirty clothes, and clutter. And since no two people's expectations are identical, this attitude has required my accepting the less than perfect standards that my children apply to their own living areas and clothes. While my house is rarely letter-perfect, it is usually presentable and I no longer waste my energy trying to sell other people on my arbitrary ideas about housekeeping.

The interesting thing to note is that if you try to be a perfectionist and think, "How could I purposely choose one thing to do imperfectly?", the chores that are left at the end of your day don't get the best of your time and energy or may even get postponed until the next day. Aren't there typically several things every day that you don't give your best because you are rushed, tired, or distracted? Why not look ahead and *plan where you can afford to perform quickly but not perfectly*, instead of letting it happen by default? It requires healthy

▼

mental balance to know in advance that you are performing less than your absolute best but appropriately to the situation, taking into account all the needs and priorities.

As you decide to let go of your compulsive need to be seen as a perfectionist, you will gain much more energy, time, and enthusiasm. You will also have the energy and desire to strike out in new directions, to discover some untapped talents, and to find new solutions to old problems.

ACTION ITEM

Find your own ways to emancipate yourself from compulsive perfectionism. Here are some examples:

- Quickly straighten your desk rather than stopping to thoroughly deal with each item.

- Write a less than perfect letter.

- Use a client's voice mail box instead of drafting a letter or waiting to talk to him or her in person.

- Do a quick partial car wash rather than a complete wash and polish.

LIFE IN THE EXPRESS LANE:

The Addictive Roar of the Crowd

66 *People in a hurry cannot think, cannot grow, nor can they decay. They are preserved in a state of perpetual puerility.* 99
—**Eric Hoffer**

66 *The trouble with life in the fast lane is that you get to the other end in an awful hurry.* 99
—**John Jensen**

66 *We can outrun the wind and the storm, but we cannot outrun the demon of Hurry.* 99
—**John Burroughs**

We hear a lot these days about being on the corporate "fast track." Many companies have special programs that identify and train their potential superstars. There are also programs for learning a language in six weeks, a musical instrument in six months, and an advanced degree in a year. Yes, our society worships the concept of speed, often for its own sake. Many of the Olympic competitions are centered on breaking a speed record. Being the youngest person ever to accomplish something is another much-applauded feat. And the *Guinness Book of World Records* is filled with people who went the farthest distance at the fastest speed.

Characteristics of "Fast-Lane" Behavior

With such widespread emphasis on speed, is it any wonder that so many of us live life in the fast lane? For devotees of this life-style, every hour is scheduled, from "power breakfasts" to negotiations over the lunch table to client-wooing dinners to late-night work sessions to work-filled weekends. This group also tends to trade in vacation time for industry conventions and conferences. In fact, fast-lane competitors go about their entire day in high gear, making quick decisions, abrupt changes, and fast moves, always in an effort to reach their destination as quickly and efficiently as possible.

Fast-lane behaviors are showing up at home, too. The family evening meal is evidence. Microwave meals and take-out fast food get the family out the door faster to soccer practice, dance lessons, committee meetings, and night courses in tax accounting. No more leisurely trips to Grandma's in the woods—we fly Grandma to the city and fit her into the schedule when there's an opening.

Does this description bring certain work partners and friends to mind? Perhaps it describes you as well. Take a moment to recall people you know who are caught in the fast lane. Can you guess what motivates them to live at such an exhilarating yet stressful and exhausting pace?

Fast-Lane Behavior

The *Lure*   is to be out in front and to beat everyone else to the prize.

The *Payoff*   is high visibility, productivity, excitement, admiration, and frequent promotions.

The *Trap*   is that the fast lane is the road to physical and psychological overload. You will tend to think more of a "quick fix" and less of a long-term investment in major changes.

Let's look at an interesting analogy to help us examine this personality type. Consider the Indianapolis 500, the major race car competition in the United States. Some of the most expensive cars in the world compete, most costing in the range of $600,000. Yet sometimes fewer than half of them are able to finish the race. That's a mere 500 miles, a distance most cars in good repair could handle with no problem. Would you be willing to pay $600,000 for a vehicle that only had a fifty-fifty chance of traveling 500 miles before breaking down?

So why are the performance records of these race cars so horrible? As compared with ordinary cars, these are built to run exclusively at top speeds. And for the vast majority of the

500-mile race they run at only one speed—full throttle. All the other gears are only used momentarily. It is rarely the super-powerful engine that breaks down, but instead a minor part, such as a ten-dollar water hose or gasket.

Dr. Larry Dossey, internationally recognized as a leader in holistic health, warns us of "Hurrysickness," a new disease rampant in the American society. Dr. Dossey describes this disease as a result of self-inflicted expectations related to our feeling that if we can only speed up enough we can finally get everything done.

We feel anxious to stay ahead, to be first, to be recognized as fastest, best, and most productive. We become addicted to the surge of adrenaline from the fast pace, the adulation of others, the sense of excitement. Soon we don't feel alive unless we have this intensity during every waking moment. The pace continues to accelerate until we become a captive of our own goals, speed, and previous records.

Our sense of urgency results in a change in our biological responses as well. Heart and respiratory rates increase, blood pressure rises, stress hormones increase—in short, our biological clocks speed up as our sense of being behind increases. The end result is frequently a "hurrysickness"

such as heart disease, high blood pressure, depression of our immune function leading to an increased susceptibility to infection and cancer, or an overactive immune system that may result in allergies, arthritis, or autoimmune diseases.

You know you have slipped into the addiction of the fast lane when you feel that you have no choice but to "run faster," achieve more in less time, and top your own goals.

If you too have many "fast-track" behaviors, you will have lots of company among other readers of this book. In fact, I occasionally succumb to this behavior pattern as well. For example, I catch myself eating lunch as though I'm vying for a prize based on how fast I can make the food disappear! I also find myself talking too rapidly, giving quick and insufficient directions, or standing at a desk making decisions and working on the phone, poised for the next leap. Sometimes I second-guess and interrupt other team members, too impatient to wait for them to finish a sentence. I get impatient in meetings, wanting quick decisions instead of group consensus discussion. Blinded by my need for speed, I don't see that quick, unthought-out decisions waste precious time later. Often the benefits of meetings come from educating the whole team and sharing perspectives so that we can move as one rather than being fractured, each with only part of the necessary information.

We may become so used to doing things at our accelerated pace that high gear is the only speed we feel comfortable in. Like the Indy cars, after a few months of operating at this speed, we experience small "mechanical failures." We begin to get headaches or sore throats, make careless errors, and have interrupted sleep. We also find ourselves stalled along the roadside by relatively insignificant obstacles, such as simple problems that we're too tired to solve. Or we create "people problems" that take more time and patience than we feel we have. Furthermore, we overlook resources, such as other team members who could assist us, because we're too busy to delegate or train them or too rushed to realize they are ready, willing, and able to help.

Breakdown, or energy overload, is the hidden danger for everyone who persists in living every waking hour at full

ACTION ITEM

Apply the race car analogy to yourself. What percentage of your day do you run in your highest gear? How often do you

- skip breakfast to save time?
- race to work, cursing every red light?
- gobble down lunch at your desk?
- hurry from assignment to assignment, overbooking yourself in an attempt to force swifter performances from yourself and your staff?
- miss office birthday celebrations and other small social functions to avoid getting behind?
- use caffeine and other stimulants to keep you alert and alcohol and sleeping pills to help you unwind?
- monitor the speed with which others accomplish their assignments and always try to finish before them?
- frequently ask your printers, programmers, and secretarial help to finish your project faster than they normally work?
- jump at every opportunity that comes your way, no matter how overextended you feel?
- finish sentences for others or interrupt with your insights?
- get impatient with complex discussions, long meetings, or social conversation in meetings?
- get frustrated with people who talk slowly, drive slowly, walk slowly, or eat slowly?

If you said yes to more than half of these questions and if you approach most aspects of your life with a "fast is best" mentality, then you have fallen victim to the energy-draining profile of a fast-laner.

throttle. Using the Indy 500 analogy again, remember that everyone needs to schedule regular pit stops—to refuel, to have a minor tune-up, and to repair worn-out parts. Yet fast-lane types are the least likely to slow down when their bodies and minds tell them to because they think that they can't spare the time. They are so consumed with getting ahead that they stop listening to their body's messages; even when their body is screaming for rest or proper nutrition or for some light-hearted fun, they keep pushing on. They frequently experience a major health crisis as a result of heroically tuning out the body's messages.

Another important element to consider is that if you are a parent, a company executive, or a leader of any kind, driving yourself beyond endurance is detrimental to others as well as yourself. As a car going out of control often crashes into other cars and causes them problems as well, you will most likely take other members of your team or family with you as you crash. Your illness will have an impact not only on your life, but on the lives of all the people around you.

What keeps fast-lane folks initially revved up is their keen sense of competition, the pressure to stay ahead, and the excitement and intensity generated by their supercharged lifestyles. But this kind of nervous energy will eventually wane as physical exhaustion and health problems take their toll. Unfortunately, divorces, poor relationships with children, career burnout, and faulty judgment come from too frenetic a pace that excludes everything and everybody that cannot keep up with the race.

Before discussing ways to switch out of high gear, we want to point out some key differences between this behavior and the high-energy patterns of children. At first glance, a child seems to be constantly in motion like our fast-lane adults. However, if you observe children more closely, you will find that they always prefer (perhaps "insist" would be a better word) to do things at their own pace, which will vary from activity to activity. Just try to hurry children through mealtime or their morning routine and see how their nature intuitively tells them to behave. In addition, children frequently switch from intense physical activity to more restful play. Young children are also much less competitive than adults. In fact, they usually don't even feel a compulsion to finish everything they begin.

But for adults, fast-lane living can be addictive as well as consuming. If you fall into this profile, the remedy is not to curb your ambitions. Rather, it is to learn to balance them with a little patience, plus the art of switching gears, in order to refuel your energy resources.

The Cure for "Fast-Lane" Behavior

The cure is *to use all your gears and to pace yourself throughout the day and week*. By knowing how to balance your high and low gears, you can restore your energy rather than deplete it each day. This skill requires an understanding of which activities genuinely call for high-gear efforts and which can be done in neutral or while idling. It also requires a sensible scheduling of projects throughout the day and week that allows changes of pace.

Do you attempt to balance the most demanding tasks with less demanding ones throughout the day? In addition, are you aware of your natural biorhythms and the times during the day when you are most alert or most fatigued? Do you plan your work day according to those normal highs and lows? Like vacationers plotting out a 1,500-mile trip, you too

can plan your work week so that you are not filled with stress and fatigue at the end of each day and work week.

Before your week begins, for example, you could consider the "route" your work will take and the difficulty of each leg of your trip. Then, with those factors in mind, you could create a work and break schedule that would allow for challenge and productivity but that wouldn't be thoroughly grueling. In addition, you could go a step further by scheduling your most difficult and stressful tasks during your most energetic times of the day, then following them with easier, more relaxing tasks. You could also follow a very stressful day with an easier one and grant yourself a relaxing night at home after a previous night burning the midnight oil. By creating a balance between high-energy exertion (loss) and times of energy restoration (gain), you can minimize your energy drains and maintain high overall energy levels.

We encourage you to begin to recognize which projects at work demand the most energy from you. Start noticing which leave you feeling the most pressured and fatigued and which make you feel the most enthusiastic and stimulated. Also notice which tasks are the most relaxing and satisfying.

Don't be like the Indy 500 race cars. Think of using not only three speeds but also reverse and neutral. In a meeting or sales call or when delegating work to a team member, if you begin with a relaxed, friendly few minutes enjoying the other person, much more can be accomplished when you get rolling with the work. When you seem to be going nowhere on a project, shift into neutral and just coast for a few minutes. Give yourself a joy break or a brief rest to refresh your mind. Think of using reverse when you realize you are off on the wrong foot or going in the wrong direction. Saying "I'm sorry" or "I was sure wrong about this. What other options might work better?" can indicate a healthy attitude for a balanced team player.

CHAPTER 12

THE
SUPERHUMAN
SYNDROME:
Retiring Your Cape

"For peace of mind, resign as general manager of the universe."

—Larry Eisenberg, *Night Light*

"It has ever been my experience that folks who have no vices have very few virtues."

—Abraham Lincoln

"What, after all, is a halo? It's only one more thing to keep clean."

—Christopher Fry

A third profile that leads to exhaustion is the superhuman syndrome. It has received a good deal of attention by the media, particularly as it relates to women geared toward careers, but it is equally applicable to men. As one who played superwoman for many years before suffering a serious case of burnout, let me describe some common patterns for this personality type.

Characteristics of the Superhuman Syndrome

The most basic underlying compulsion for superhumans is to be all things to all people. A typical male superhuman will strive to achieve maximum success at his job while maintaining a high profile in his community. He might also attempt to have quality time with his spouse and children each day. We might find him serving as an officer in the Chamber of Commerce, leading his son's Boy Scout troop, volunteering to work for every United Way fund-raising campaign, supervising a monthly neighborhood cleanup, and scheduling a major home fix-up project every summer, doing the work himself. He may also feel somewhat responsible for the well-being of his friends and staff. Thus he frequently invites his divorced brother over to dinner, his widowed secretary out to lunch, and his neighbor's "problem child" over to the house for motivational talks. He rarely has a relaxing lunch by himself or a jog alone around the park because he reasons that he can use that time to meet a potential client or teach his son another football maneuver.

Similarly, the superwoman usually holds a full-time job while going to night school three evenings a week to advance her career opportunities. Of course she still expects her house to look as spick-and-span as during the five years she stayed at home to raise the children, so she spends at least ten hours each week cleaning house. She continues to teach the Sunday School class she has led for eight years, she manages to make homemade Christmas presents and goodies for most of her relatives, and she serves on the executive committees of Planned Parenthood and a local art museum. She also takes an active part in her children's school activities, plants an extensive flower garden each spring, plays Sunday-night bridge with her husband and friends, and relishes her role as an always-available friend to a growing number of women. Every spare minute is spent ministering to the many needs of her children, husband, aging parents, employees, and friends.

When I recall the story of Superman, I am amazed at how much of it I have unconsciously internalized. Remember the story and think about the message being conveyed between the lines.

Superman was a baby sent to Earth in a spaceship because his planet was about to blow up. There weren't enough resources for his parents to escape, so they sent their baby to the safety of Earth. He was found in a pasture in the Midwest. The farmer's wife made his famous suit out of the blanket from his home planet, Krypton.

In the years that followed, Superman never spilled gravy on his front (or if he did, it magically disappeared). He never had a run in his tights, nor did they bag around the knees like mine do. He never had sweat rings under his arms in spite of his breathtaking heroics. Even if there were seven crimes going on at the same time, Superman somehow solved them all singlehandedly. *He never asked for help.*

Superman only existed when he was leaping tall buildings with a single bound or was more powerful than a locomotive. The rest of the time, he changed into mild-mannered (read boring) Clark Kent, so average that Lois Lane looked right past him.

What does this comic book story teach us? I never thought it did more than entertain until I began to notice the messages and the parallels to my own behavior. Let's look at some of the hidden messages:

- You only exist when you are rescuing others or performing miraculous feats.

- You are lovable only when you achieve superhuman performance.

- Time away from the job is for mere mortals. (Superman never took a stroll, had a sweetie, went on a picnic.)

- Asking others for help is beneath your dignity.

- Being dressed impeccably is part of your image and mythical power.

- Be strong. Don't cry. Don't reveal weakness. Be perfect. Have all the answers. Thrive on solving the impossible 100 percent of the time. Have no imperfections—ever. Have no life or time for yourself. Be bigger than life.

Most of these messages are false. Learning to accept yourself and others, learning to live in balance and be part of a team rather than the sole hero, are key ingredients in achieving mental health and balance.

Many of our parental roles are another version of superhuman. We blame ourselves for anything and everything that goes wrong for our children. We can't see that their problems are their opportunities to grow and learn. Stepping back and trusting children to find their own solutions, then allowing them to live with the consequences of their decisions, results in healthier, happier, more balanced families and more responsible children.

Superhumans are extremely outer-directed, sensitive, and responsive to the needs and requests of others but have long since lost touch with their own inner needs and messages. Instead of prioritizing their concerns and interests and limiting their involvements, they rarely say no to any request made of them—which means they rarely have a moment to spare for their individual needs and interests.

On the outside, Schweitzer, Mead, and Edison appear to exhibit the superhuman syndrome as well. They involved themselves in a number of diverse activities and led very busy lives. But they learned how to *balance* their energy by scheduling time each day to rest and be alone, absorbed in an activity of their own choosing rather than constantly pouring their energy out to one recipient after another. They frequently lost themselves in a "timeless" joy, just for the fun of it. This provided them with private, personal satisfaction and creativity, which are sources of mental and emotional energy. Moreover, they knew how to balance their tasks and activities rather than spreading themselves too thin by constantly piling one new endeavor on top of another. Superhumans, on the other hand, get *out of balance,* doing everything possible for others while leaving almost no time to tend to their personal needs.

Finally, Schweitzer, Mead, and Edison had a gift of inspiring and encouraging others to be a vital part of their team. They served as mentors and coaches to an energetic team of young protégés. Each benefited from the energy and accomplishments of a committed and inspired team.

The Superhuman Syndrome

The *Lure*   is be everyone's hero!

The *Payoff*   is to feel needed, vital, well liked, and admired.

The *Trap*   is having all your energy lapped up by an endless procession of causes and people, which will ultimately result in, you guessed it, *burnout.*

It might help to examine the reasons underlying the superhuman syndrome. I confess that I foolishly struggled "heroically" to play this role for many years. I'm sure my first mentor was the comic-book hero for whom this syndrome is named. The two and one-half years I commuted to Columbia University in New York while teaching full time and raising my son in Dallas made up one of the most "heroic"—and hectic and exhausting—times of my life. My list of roles included:

- much-admired single mother who was actively involved in my son's life;

- full-time associate professor who was always available to my university students (I carried a double teaching load of graduate students and directed a major research project involving 5,500 children, teachers, and parents);

- doctoral student aiming to make excellent grades and to complete my program in record time;

- community worker involved in women's groups, religious education, the Children's Medical Center Psychiatric Program, the Texas Scottish Rite's research on dyslexic children, and eleven other community research projects;

- gardener with a thriving flower garden;

- single homemaker who frequently hosted get-togethers for friends and graduate students;

- problem solver to an average of eight to ten students;

- attentive daughter to my parents; and

- recipient of an award as an outstanding professor at Southern Methodist University the same year I completed my doctorate with high honors.

"How can you manage to do it all so well?" was the comment I often got from my neighbors, friends, and work associates. Since I was held in such high esteem, I totally believed in the superhuman role I was playing. At the time, I wouldn't dare let anyone down by (shudder!) passing up a challenge or simply referring someone's request for help to another resource. Like Superman, I was so used to giving to others that I rarely gave myself permission to receive from others without wanting to outdo their favor in return! For instance, if a neighbor brought me a covered dish when I was sick, I felt compelled to return the dish with a fresh-baked casserole in it. A gracious "thank you" was insufficient for the likes of me. Translating this situation to the work force, superhumans might attempt to cut their operational budget by 10 percent even though they have been asked to cut it only 2 percent, or they might write a fifty-page report when a ten-page report would do.

With the exceedingly full and diversified lives that most of us lead, the large number of roles we try to fill is not highly unusual. People who are adept at establishing a healthy give-and-take between these roles and their personal energy needs can manage to maintain most of them. But I, like other super-human hopefuls, tried to perform each role to the best of my ability, which led to my ultimate undoing. If I had been energy conscious, I would have cut back on the number of social and household duties I fulfilled during my very demanding two and one-half years of commuting between Dallas and New York. I could have decided to clean house only every other week. I could have taught my son how to make ten-minute dinners and relied on the most nutritious of the frozen dinners available for half our meals. And I could have let the flower garden go one year, or cut back to planting only a tiny garden. I could have delayed the home renovation projects. I could have shifted my entertaining to be more casual—a covered dish rather than me preparing a five-course meal for twelve people, for example. And I could have encouraged the long list of people coming to me for lengthy listening and support sessions to seek qualified counseling, freeing me to enjoy time with my family and friends instead of always performing a service.

Kay Russell, one of our team members, formed a creative group with three friends when they all were homemakers with small children. To make their hectic lives more fun, they planned frequent lunches and all pitched in for an hour and cleaned house or accomplished a similar "un-fun" chore for the hostess before lunch (a shared covered-dish affair). Meanwhile their eight children enjoyed playing, with one mom supervising. They also traded out child care for each other, using playful "coupons" for number of children, hours kept, and so forth. The

ACTION ITEM

To what extent do you play the superhuman role? Check (✔) each statement that describes you.

☐   I rarely have a minute to myself.

☐   I find it very difficult, if not impossible, to say no to a worthy cause or person requesting my involvement.

☐   I frequently try to solve everyone's problems. `

☐   I heroically drag myself to a sales meeting with the flu and a 103-degree temperature rather than delegate the job to a junior member of the team.

☐   I receive a constant string of phone calls all weekend long.

☐   I always do it myself rather than ask for assistance or cut back on my responsibilities.

☐   I feel compelled to find ways to make anything I do better than ever before.

☐   In coaching my child's soccer team, I insist on winning instead of encouraging the kids to learn and enjoy the game.

If you answered yes to more than half, you may be stretching yourself very thin among work, family, social, professional, and academic responsibilities.

toddlers are now in college, and all four families still thrive on eighteen-plus years of creative friendship.

Instead of choosing any of these possible alternatives, superhumans often try to maintain their normal roles and commitments while expanding their schedule into eighty and ninety hours per week of work and traveling combined with their already busy schedule. By sleeping less, relaxing less, eating on the run, and skipping meals, they push and push themselves. They become mentally, emotionally, and physically exhausted. They also tend to look for new causes to pursue rather than taking care of their own personal needs and areas of growth.

Surprisingly, a person with low self-esteem often lies behind this profile. The superhuman typically does not call on others for help because of the need to be needed. Perhaps this life-style leads to the most out-of-balance scenario of them all. As superhumans pile more and more activities and rescue missions onto their agenda, they have less time to do each activity well. They end up rushing through everything so hurriedly that they actually get less pleasure from each task they accomplish and each person they spend time with. And ironically, the more they do, the more they feel pressured to do.

Once you have established this pattern of behavior and these dependencies in your life, it is very difficult to change (and to disappoint all those people counting on you, you might be thinking). But in the long run, you will be doing everyone a favor.

The Cure for the Superhuman Syndrome

The cure is *reciprocity,* which refers to balance—an equal give and take—between two people. That's a difficult lesson to learn, knowing why and how to invite a mutual exchange of time and services from others and promoting interdependence instead of dependence. It involves taking off the hero's cape and becoming a balanced person again.

When my mentor Jerry Spalding, a management consultant in Dallas, first asked me to do the kind of objective assessment found in the Action Item on the following page, I felt rather offended at having to rate the qualities of each friendship as if I were comparing the rates and policies of a lending institution! After all, I wasn't being kind and helpful to all these people with the expectation of their repaying me in a like manner. Yet Jerry taught me how to create a much more mature and fulfilling type of relationship with others. He showed me that when I was not requesting an equal amount of assistance and strength back from others, I was allowing them to neglect their own inner resources. I was also denying them the satisfaction of giving something of equal value back to me. This is called "learned dependence," and I was teaching this quality left and right without realizing it.

I now realize how damaging it can be to encourage others to become dependent on me rather than to develop their own

ACTION ITEM

First ask yourself, among all the people you are giving to, which ones would you also like to receive something back from? Your children, spouse, or friends? Your work associates? On a separate piece of paper, quickly jot down the names or initials of the people you spend the most time with each week. Then beside each name rate the quality of that relationship. Use a plus sign (+) to indicate that you receive more than you give to that person, a check mark (✔) to indicate that you have a fairly balanced give-and-take relationship of helping each other and listening supportively, or a minus sign (–) to indicate that you are primarily the supporter of that person's needs. For example, if you walk or carpool with a friend twice a week, are the conversations dominated by your friend's problems and concerns or by yours? Or is there an equal give and take of topics that are helpful for both of you?

Next, take steps to bring balance to your list. You might choose to spend less time with some of your constantly-in-crisis friends. Instead, look for a few mentors to add support and positive fun to your life. Learn to ask for what you want in advance.

sense of confidence and self-reliance. What I had created with many people was a guardianship relationship, with me as the center of power and wisdom. It led them to rely on someone else to "leap tall buildings" instead of learning how to scale their own obstacles, no matter how long it took. In contrast, Jerry taught me to develop win-win relationships. I became their coach rather than their guardian angel by encouraging them to begin solving their own problems. Ultimately, this type of "empowering," or "enabling," relationship results in many mini-heros learning to be team players rather than one superhero flying above all the rest. Jerry also taught me the importance of developing a few friendships with people to whom I could look for help and support. He became one of those significant friends and mentors.

Develop the following habits to cure your superhuman syndrome:

1. Listen to others.

2. Empower their strengths. Match your weaknesses with the strengths of others.
3. Become a coach instead of just a hero.
4. Ask for help *in advance*.
5. Become open and vulnerable.
6. Go off-duty frequently and pass the baton.

One way you can help yourself get out of the superhuman syndrome and help others at the same time is to share the opportunities that come your way. Instead of trying to do everything yourself, keep a list of people who are rarely called upon for help and ask them to help you. I began a list of the elderly, graduate students, international students and immigrants, individuals with handicaps, teenagers, and other young people who are often overlooked but have a great deal to share. When an opportunity comes along that I do not have time for, I ask someone on the list to take my place. By making referrals I have learned to feel good about bringing new opportunities to deserving people. It has been a real win-win-win situation. I can feel good because I am no longer overextended. The group gets a well-prepared, highly enthusiastic speaker or teacher. And the person giving the presentation enjoys the process.

Another true example of reciprocity in the work force comes from one of our Energy Engineering seminars. An executive secretary explained that her desk was located close to the copier machine. Employees expected her to help them with every problem that arose with the equipment, which on some days left little time for her own work. She admitted that she enjoyed feeling needed and being praised as "the only one who could work miracles with the copier." But this role became too time-consuming. And since she had allowed everyone to become dependent upon her, she knew it was her responsibility to teach others to share the burden with her.

Her solution was to make a chart of all the types of problems she was called upon to correct. As each problem arose, she added it to a list. She then invited the person she was helping learn the procedure to sign his or her name next to the problem. The next time that problem arose, the woman told the person needing help to turn to any name listed beside it. Her biggest challenge was to resist the plea for immediate help and politely yet firmly refer to the list. Within a few weeks she had trained a large staff to be both self-reliant and team-motivated when it came to dealing with the copier. And she stopped letting others constantly sap her flow of energy and concentration. She had taught the valuable lesson of *reciprocity*.

One facet of reciprocity that is often difficult for the superhuman to accept is that you must trust other people to do their jobs and relinquish control of some situations. Ben Bradlee, legendary editor of the *Washington Post*, described how

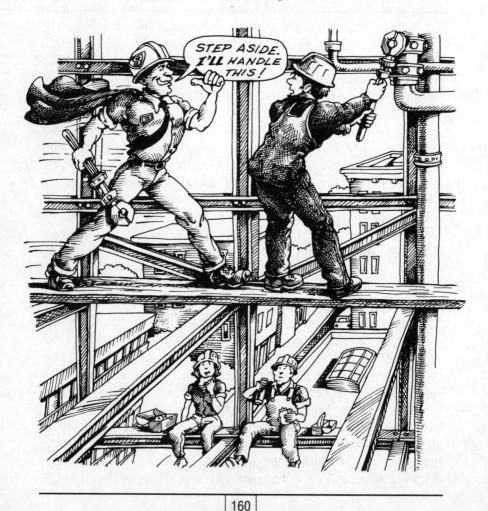

▼

he created a great newspaper: "You lead, you inspire. The first thing you do is hire. You surround yourself with the most talented, intelligent, and delightful people you can find, and you let them do their jobs. . . . Leave them to it!"

In other chapters we will provide many more examples of creating reciprocal, energy-sharing relationships with co-workers, friends, and family members. But for now, look at your list of relationships in the last Action Item. Put a star by those that are sapping more energy than they are giving back. Then rest assured that within one to three months of patient but firm coaching, you will be able to teach these people how to have energy-sharing relationships with you rather than energy-draining ones. When doing this, consider author Wayne Dyer's statement: "People treat us the way we teach them to treat us."

Now that I am learning to limit my roles and balance my commitment to each activity, I am delighted to find that my accomplishments and friendships are more special than they were before. I don't have the uncontrollable urge or even the burning desire to involve myself with everything that crosses my path. But by wisely managing my energy resources, I do have the time and motivation to participate in many select areas of life. And now that I have stopped teaching "learned helplessness" in favor of self-reliance and independence, my relationships are much more rewarding and energizing.

**"People treat us the way
we teach them to treat us."**

—Wayne Dyer

THE CURE FOR BURNOUT:

Learning to Refuel Your Tank

> 66 *You don't grow old. You get old by not growing.* 99
>
> —**E. Stanley Jones, minister**

> 66 *Making a living is necessary and often satisfying; eventually, making a difference becomes more important.* 99
>
> —**David Campbell, author and Vice President, Center for Creative Leadership**

> 66 *Be not afraid of life. Believe life is worth living, and your belief will help create the fact.* 99
>
> —**William James, "The Will to Believe"**

ortunately, it usually takes a lot longer to get yourself into burnout than it does to get yourself back into balance. The key is to know your own symptoms. And the earlier you recognize the symptoms, the less time you will spend in a drained, burned-out position.

Our research has found at least twelve key life-style factors affecting energy. There may be other factors that affect you. Be open to your own sense of what is best for you. Descriptions of these twelve energy factors and their significance follow. Rate yourself on each of these factors, using the self-test at the end of the chapter. Then pick the one factor that is most important for improving your energy and gently increase the amount of attention you give to this factor. For each of the following ask yourself, "What percentage of the time do I get an adequate amount of this?"

Proper Rest

R. Buckminster Fuller, Pablo Picasso, Thomas Edison, Margaret Mead, and many other geniuses were known for their unusual sleep habits. They accommodated their unique needs, slept whenever and wherever they needed to, and invested an intense passion and joy in both work and play. Under different circumstances, our need for sleep and rest will vary. Sometimes changing to play or pleasure will renew us more than sleep. The secret is to listen to your body. Rest when it asks you to rest. The second secret is to enjoy both your work and your play with equal commitment.

Peter Hauri, director of the Insomnia Program at the Mayo Clinic, reported: "When human beings are placed in an underground cave with artificial light, plenty of food, but no clock, they still maintain a circadian rhythm." Not all people need the same amount of sleep. Hauri noted that some adults sleep three hours a night or less without problems while others sleep ten to twelve hours and feel deprived it they get less.

Eating for High Performance and Peak Energy

We know generally that too much salt, sugar, fat, cholesterol, and caffeine will lower performance levels. They interfere with the chemistry of your brain and impede optimum performance, and they can plug up your cardiovascular system, causing your heart to pump harder, your body to get less oxygen, and toxins in your blood to be less effectively filtered out.

We also know now that salt, sugar, fat, and caffeine are addictive. The more you eat, the more you want. And the more salt you add to your food, the less you taste it, so the more salt you want. These are called soft addictions, but they work in much the same way as the hard addictions of nicotine, alcohol, and narcotics. They have the most control in your life when you are out of balance. So getting your life back into balance can be an important first step toward eliminating these soft addictions from your eating habits.

Caffeine stimulates the central nervous system and can produce a variety of effects elsewhere in the body. Depending upon how much you consume, it can increase your heartbeat, speed up your metabolism, and promote secretion of stomach acid. Psychologically, the effect of caffeine has been described as a "lift." However, you won't feel more pep when you drink your coffee, but instead will feel worse without it. To get the most benefit from your daily coffee, you need to keep your daily limit to two cups or less.

Other studies indicate that coffee and tea, even if decaffeinated, act as a diuretic. As such, they flush out significant chemicals from your system that are necessary for your brain to function most effectively. So drinking six to eight glasses of water daily (which increases significant chemicals to the brain) can be as positive for your energy and productive thinking as a heavy coffee habit can be draining and debilitating.

What percentage of the time do you enjoy eating for energy or good nutrition? (You may notice that we purposely avoid the term "diet" because to us it has the negative connotation of being deprived or not eating what you might prefer. We think it is essential that you link positive words to your food and drink choices. So you pick the terms—eating for energy, eating clean, eating for high performance—whatever motivates you to make healthy choices for yourself.)

Think of the changes in your eating habits as permanent rather than as a temporary diet. When you decide to gently improve your eating habits for life, you begin to make real progress. The secret is to find many ways to have fun other than eating junk food. Exercise daily. (This changes your metabolism so that you think better and process your food in more productive ways.)

Another secret is to buy and bring into the house only energy food. For example, make sure that there are always plenty of fresh, appetizing fruits and vegetables in the house. Instead of an alcoholic or soft drink beverage, try a cool glass of sparkling water with a twist of lime in the evening. Whole-grain breads with high fiber round out meals. Steamed vegetables can be an alternative to meat, and fruit for dessert is a nice change. One key is to make sure you enjoy and look forward to your food choices. Fresh raspberries in season and snow peas can become a regular treat. Even though we make sure we always have plenty of fresh fruits and vegetables, our food bills have decreased a lot. Even artichokes and fresh blueberries cost less than sirloin steak or a gallon of ice cream—and are much healthier for you. Be sure your meals are balanced, and slowly try some changes to see what fits you best.

We also use this idea in our office. We take turns bringing fresh fruit for snacks. We limit the coffee and enjoy mint tea most mornings, and we find that keeping a glass of water in front of us encourages us to drink more water and less caffeine. When we focus on the energy benefits and reward ourselves for positive choices (and waste no energy feeling guilty when we backslide), we keep moving forward. The more we mentally link energy with eating choices, the easier it becomes to make good choices.

Daily "Nonstressed," Fun Aerobic Exercise

Probably a minimum of twenty to forty minutes a day of nonstressed aerobic exercise is needed to bring your mind and body back to optimum. To be aerobic, you need to get your heart rate up to 120 beats per minute and keep it there for a minimum of twenty minutes. Another easy gauge is to exercise hard enough to sweat. The American Heart Association suggests the following target heart rate formula: subtract your age from 220. This is your average maximum heart rate. Your target zone is 60 to 75 percent of your average maximum heart rate. (Multiply your average maximum heart rate by .60 to .75.) Sustain your target zone rate for fifteen to thirty minutes three times a week.

In the past eleven years, a new medical field has emerged that links our moods, attitudes, thoughts, and body chemistry. Called psychoneuroimmunology, this field provides a scientific explanation for the positive effects produced by the "power of positive thinking." As Janet Hopson points out in the July 1988 issue of *Psychology Today,* thoughts actually alter body chemistry by changing the levels of hormones, endorphins, and other key chemicals that affect the brain, the immune system, and subsequently our perception of energy. We therefore believe it is important to choose to *enjoy* exercise. If you get up early to run but are reminding yourself all the while that you don't like it, you are blocking the beneficial effects of endorphins with your negative attitude.

I find that I need lots of different ways to enjoy daily aerobics. I tap dance, jog, and power walk with friends and clients, swim, polka dance on weekends, Jazzercise, and jump rope. I buy colorful gear, use energizing music, and search out parks, malls, lakes, and other appealing places to exercise.

One of our favorite client stories is of a women's group that went on a two-mile aerobic walk and came back exhausted. Their coach encouraged them to walk the next day as if they were five-year-olds. They took turns playing follow-the-leader, skipping, giggling, and acting however they felt. This time they walked *five miles* and came back truly invigorated. Look for creative ways to make *your* exercise this appealing.

Time Alone

Know that each of us is different in this personal need, which may vary from time to time. In thinking back over your normal current pattern, how would you rate your need for time alone? Both highly creative people and people who are unusually productive seem to require some significant time to be alone with their own thoughts. This may be part of their morning jogging routine, or they may plan quiet time alone when they get up early or are the first to arrive at their work place.

Teaching children to treasure and use time alone not only helps them develop a valuable lifelong habit that can lead to balance and high performance but also helps them understand a parent's need for precious alone time on a daily basis.

Time to Read and Learn

It's easy to get so busy that you feel as though you have no time to read and learn. Yet these are times when we may be spinning our wheels and not even be aware of it. Taking the time on a daily basis to glean new ideas—new food for thought and inspiration—is just as important as enjoying regular, nutritious meals. Henry Ford once said, "A man who doesn't read is no better off than a man who can't read."

As you consider how to make this happen for yourself within a busy schedule, think of the variety of reading spots available. You might try keeping magazines by your bed or in the den (to read during TV commercials) or the bathroom. A smaller collection could go in your briefcase.

How often do you pick something that is sheer fun or fantasy to read, just for entertainment? *The Velveteen Rabbit, The Hobbit, The Little Prince,* or other children's books can entice you away from stress and pressure and renew your spirit. Dr. Seuss had a wonderful way of doing this for us. Go to a library and head for the children's section. Or choose a novel or engaging volume of history to take you away from the frantic pace.

Spiritual Growth

Do you have daily habits to fill your need for spiritual growth? Are you aware that there are stages of development in your spiritual life just as there are in your physical life? You may fill this need by daily devotional or inspirational reading or by meditation and prayer. You may focus on a collection of inspirational poems or take walks in nature.

Robert Greenleaf's *The Servant as Leader* describes the paradox of being able to serve those you lead as an essential quality of leadership. This can be seen by looking at the examples of Jesus, Buddha, Gandhi, and other great leaders. Do you regularly take care of this aspect of your life so that you can be a steady and trustworthy role model? How often do you find daily time to focus on your own spiritual growth?

Intimacy and Love

The only other time besides childhood when we feel so alive and filled with energy is when we fall madly in love and are courting. This is a time when we give ourselves permission to play and be childlike. Think about how that permission affects your energy.

I remember being in my mid-forties and hopelessly in love with Larry. I worked long hours, then rushed home to clean house, fix a lovers' meal by the fireside, arrange flowers, and spiff myself up. We would enjoy long walks in the moonlight and get up at 5:00 A.M. to see each other daily. And I would stay up until all hours writing poetry. I got far less sleep yet had far more energy. What was the secret?

We were devoting lots of time, energy, and creativity into pleasing each other and playing together. We shared feelings and secrets, and risked playing in lots of little-kid ways. Going barefoot in the mud, fishing in the rain, flying kites—all kinds of foolishness were suddenly wonderful because they were shared with someone special.

We suspect that the chemical changes that happen in our brain and body have a tremendous impact on personal energy. Notice that as we marry and shift back into routine, adult, unimaginative behavior, we lose that energy bonus.

When you are courting, you put a lot of time and attention into pleasing your lover. And in the process, there is a synergy as your lover also tries to find ways to please you. It is important to let your lover know what you want or like. Playing keep-away and not disclosing your deepest wishes, then feeling hurt when your partner can't read your mind, is a sure way to drain your energy and relationship.

Why not make time to meet with your special someone and make a long list of things you would enjoy doing? Then schedule some delicious fun into each day, each evening, and each weekend.

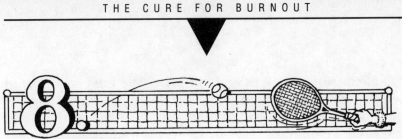

Fun, Joy, and Play

If this only happens "when you have time," let us recommend a great book to you. Written by a young, creative father and minister, Tim Hansel, *When I Relax I Feel Guilty* can be an enormously freeing resource for you.

Are you waiting until you "finish all your work before you go out to play"? That was good advice for you as a child, when your work could be finished in forty-five minutes or an hour. Yet now, if you were to finish everything there is for you to do—at work, at home, in the community, in your extended family—it would take several lifetimes. As a responsible, creative adult, the more you accomplish, the more there is that needs to be done. Play, fun, and joy can provide the energy needed for work. So we need to rephrase the above rule to read "Plan your joy as thoughtfully and as frequently as you plan your work," or "Be sure to balance your work with refreshing, invigorating play." Many of us haven't played for so long that it is truly difficult to think of doing so, much less knowing how. What percentage of the time do you get enough fun, joy, and play to keep you refreshed, joyful, and energized?

Quality Time with Family and Friends

You might notice a magical energy burst when you are around kids and you let yourself become a kid again. Any grandparent will know what I mean. If you have small children of your own, set aside time to enjoy them and let yourself be energized by becoming one of them.

Debbie Bittick, a busy single mother who holds a top position in finance and administration with Brown & Root Power, told of driving with her five-year-old daughter, who was filled with questions and curiosity. The busy mom heard herself begin a reprimand: "Brittany, if you don't stop bugging me with your questions, I'm going to . . ." Then she caught herself and continued, ". . . put your nose on your toes!" Her daughter laughed and countered, "I'm going to put your elbow on your foot!" Instead of getting frustrated, the mother shifted to playful humor in place of a hurtful reprimand, and made the trip fun for both of them.

Part of the reason for lack of quality time with friends and family is that we often don't plan the time we spend with them. We just show up tired and slightly grumpy and wait to see what happens. What if you start by brainstorming a list of possibilities for enjoyment over the next few months? Larry and I dreamed up the idea of having a two-person art show at a local gallery, giving away our paintings just for the fun of it. The idea grew and in the process we found ourselves doing two or three paintings each week in time that used to be wasted in tiredness. Our grown kids decided to come home for the show. One of the best aspects of this project was that we created some of the paintings together. When one of us became discouraged, the other finished the painting. These combined efforts capture Larry's lovely, more traditional landscape and impressionistic style along with my eclectic patterns and abstract style.

Every family has members with talents. Think of ways to involve other family members as you explore and expand these talents. Use your time with your family and friends to enjoy the uniqueness of the people closest to you rather than giving them time only when you are exhausted.

New Interests and Old Hobbies

Many busy people have long since given up hobbies and time-consuming outside interests as something that doesn't fit their life-style. Yet in our research, we noted that most high-energy people typically have many hobbies and outside interests that feed new energy and insights into each other.

We encourage each participant in our Energy Engineering seminars to explore some new interests or even some old hobbies once enjoyed but given up as too time-consuming. Give yourself permission to start but not finish a hobby. Often something that looks as if it would be enjoyable turns out not to be. Try out many possibilities so that you can discover the few that do fit you.

Perhaps you have a kit or hobby in your closet that you started but lost interest in, and now you refuse to start another hobby until that one is finished. Give it away on the next birthday or anniversary that comes up: "Here's a great quilt, and it's already started for you. Such a deal!!!" Or give it to charity or a home for the elderly. Someone would love to pick up where you lost interest, and you need to emancipate your-self from this guilt trap and move on to new possibilities. This is where we get confused and apply our work habits ("Finish what you start. Be persistent and disciplined. Follow the rules.") to our play. If instead you let the little kid in you do it his or her own way, you will unleash a whole new level of energy and creativity.

One power plant superintendent who now spends many happy evenings designing stained glass mandalas and build-ing unique kaleidoscopes told us how he discovered the im-portance of daily time for joy breaks and play: "It has saved my life . . . if not physically, then mentally."

If you are not sure where to begin on this but know that you could benefit by discovering some new, exciting outside interests, you might start with a trip to the library. Or try hob-by shops, craft shops, or sporting goods/outdoor recreation stores. Don't stick to the norms. Some men have discovered that they are good at needlepoint or stitchery; women may enjoy hobbies typically seen as male-oriented, such as carpen-try or rock-climbing.

How often do you allow yourself to enjoy refreshing, renewing immersion in outside interests or hobbies? It is interesting to note that throughout history many of the major contributions and breakthroughs came from people's hobbies rather than from their vocations. The Wright brothers ran a bicycle shop but had a passion for flying. Here again is the link of passion and play to significant mental contributions. Copernicus was an amateur astronomer. Ben Franklin, Thomas Jefferson, and many others made major contributions out of love for their hobbies while making their living in other, more conventional areas.

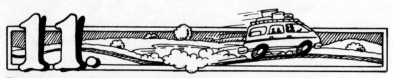

Regular and Frequent Vacations

Have you ever known yourself or others to finally take a vacation and then have trouble letting go and truly relaxing? Perhaps this takes the form of needing to stay on schedule instead of allowing yourself to do what you feel like doing when you feel like it.

Being on vacation calls for a different type of thinking and response. Often it is more important to switch into these responses than to geographically be in a certain spot. By practicing "being on vacation," even if it's only for twenty minutes or two hours a weekend, we can keep ourselves refreshed and renewed.

The idea of regular vacations led us to find a way to make a small part of every business trip a vacation of sorts. We find that calling it a mini-vacation helps to remind us and others of its purpose. We might take a twenty-minute side trip through a craft boutique or a historic area, or plan an extra day to hike through a wilderness area. It takes preplanning and this, we find, is a big part of the secret. If we creatively keep work integrated with refreshing joy breaks, we work with more energy, productivity, and creative problem solving. Indeed, we find that we get more done of higher quality in less time with more time and energy left to enjoy other dimensions of our life! We know our life is in balance when we are as excited to get back to work as we were to leave on vacation. This, after all, is one of the primary goals of Energy Engineering. What percentage of time do you get enough regular and frequent vacations to keep you refreshed and at your best?

Sense of Purpose

The health care profession is learning that a sense of purpose in one's life is not only key to having vital energy and motivation but perhaps to continuing to live. Statistics indicate that within two years of retirement, if one hasn't replaced career purpose with some new purpose or commitment, frequently health fails and in some cases life ends. Pleasure alone does not seem to be enough to energize life. Purpose and a sense of making a difference is essential.

The idea of retirees who simply sit and rock and rot is out of date. In 1989's *Money Magazine's Guide to Personal Finance,* Lani Luciano wrote, "Don't forget what's potentially your most productive retirement asset: yourself." Luciano encouraged people to cultivate any activity they enjoy that can provide fun, a sense of purpose, additional income, and a lot of options as they head into retirement.

Abraham Maslow, in *The Farther Reaches of Human Nature,* regards purpose as the key to life and explains how a sense of purpose differentiates what he calls "self-actualizing people": "self-actualizing individuals (more matured, more fully human), by definition, already suitably gratified in their basic needs, are now motivated in other higher ways, to be called metamotivations. . . . in all cases . . . they are dedicated people, devoted to some task 'outside themselves,' some vocation, or duty, or beloved job. . . . something for which the person is a 'natural,' something that he is suited for . . . even something that he was born for. . . . The dichotomizing of work and play is transcended." Maslow thought purpose was so essential to the quality of life that he developed his theory of metamotivation.

Midlife crisis is a classic example of what happens to our energy when focus and purpose are lost. When we begin to realize that we won't live forever and maybe won't ever reach our goal of being CEO of the company (or whatever our life-

ACTION ITEM

The Cure: Refueling Your Tank

What percentage of the time do you get an adequate amount of each of these?

	0	10	20	30	40	50	60	70	80	90	100%
1. Proper rest											
2. Good nutrition											
3. Daily "nonstressed" exercise											
4. Time alone											
5. Time to read and learn											
6. Spiritual growth											
7. Intimacy and love											
8. Fun, joy, and play											
9. Quality time with family and friends											
10. New interests or hobbies											
11. Regular and frequent vacations											
12. Sense of purpose											

Choose one area that is low and creatively brainstorm some ways to increase the time devoted to this area by 10 percent over the next month. The purpose in setting a modest goal is to be sure it is attainable. Set yourself up to win. Let both your intuition and your logic tell you which is most important to improve. Frequently, a small improvement in one critical area can make a big difference toward moving you back to whole-brained balance.

dream has been), we may go into a depression. The "empty nest" syndrome is another form of losing touch with our identity. Depression is often linked to lack of exciting dreams or goals. When we feel limited and boxed in, a victim of our current circumstances, we can suffer from an overwhelming loss of energy and loss of general enthusiasm for life.

Getting back in touch with dreams or coming up with new purpose can renew energy and zest for life. Going back to school, starting your own business, writing a book, taking up a new hobby, getting started on a fitness program, learning a foreign language and planning a trip to use it, taking a leadership role in a community project, renewing your spiritual growth—all this has to do with the importance of purpose in boosting personal energy.

In reflecting on these twelve factors, you may be painfully aware that what you know you should do for yourself is far away from the daily choices you make. Why don't we exercise daily, make healthy food choices, quit smoking, and devote quality time to our family? You may think lack of time is the reason, but it's often just an excuse.

Abraham Maslow calls clinging to our weaknesses the Jonah Complex. This is the tendency to run away from the opportunities to rise to our highest potential. As he explains in *The Farther Reaches of Human Nature,* "We fear our highest possibilities. . . . We enjoy and even thrill to the godlike possibilities we see in ourselves. . . . And yet we simultaneously shiver with weakness, awe, and fear before these very same possibilities."

Enormous energy can be consumed in avoiding these opportunities as well as grieving for the roads not taken. The self-assessment in the Action Item can help you reflect on where you are holding yourself back and where you can make significant gains through moving toward balance.

AUCTION TODAY

14

FOUR STEPS TO NEW ENERGY:

The "Big E"

> 66 All of the animals excepting man know that the principal business of life is to enjoy it. 99
>
> —**Samuel Butler,** *Note-books*

> 66 The way I see it, if you want the rainbow, you gotta put up with the rain. 99
>
> —**Dolly Parton**

> 66 Achievers know that creativity comes not from sitting alone in the dark but from just the opposite, from being out in the world, from finding bits of genius to put in combination with ordinary problems. . . . the achiever listens to the chorus of accomplishments past but hears original melodies. 99
>
> —**Dale Dauten,** *Taking Chances*

arly into our work on energy, we stumbled onto a rather basic approach to what we now call Energy Engineering. It began simply by observing what gave us energy and what drained our energy. We each made our own list and each was different. One of our lists looked something like the one shown in the diagram.

+	−
What Gives Me Energy	**What Drains My Energy**
bright colors	waiting in lines
interesting people	arguments
certain music	routine work
most art	paperwork
unusual items	tedium
humor	traffic
well-designed clothes	excessive structure
flowers	guilt
sincere compliments	worry

Four Energy-Building Steps

1. **Observe what gives you energy and what drains your
    energy.** This can change according to the circumstances
    and the time of day, so it can be helpful to train yourself
    to become aware of your energy flow. Sam Farber sold
    Copco Inc. in anticipation of a retirement spent dabbling
    in art and art history, but he quickly realized that his
    energy was drained by retirement. While looking for
    something else to do, he noticed that his wife, who suf-
    fered from arthritis, was having difficulty operating kitch-
    en gadgets. Soon Oxo International was a reality. Farber
    began work on user-friendly kitchen tools designed for
    the elderly and people with handicaps. He found a de-
    signer who agreed to become a part of his team in ex-
    change for a royalty, and the Good Grips line debuted at
    a show in 1990—at that first show, $750,000 worth of or-
    ders were written. Farber has given up the idea of retire-
    ment. He says he's far too excited about his new project
    to even consider quitting work now.

2. **Block unnecessary energy loss.** If "guilt" or "worry" are
    on your list of energy drains, let's start by simply letting
    go of these two behaviors. They do nothing to help your
    productivity. When we are children, guilt helps us know
    when we are out of bounds. We have a strong right brain
    (the basis for feelings and guilt) but not a well-developed
    left brain (the basis for ethics and rational, abstract judg-
    ment). Guilt protects and warns us until we are older and
    can use judgment and logic to guide our behavior. Notice
    how often guilt is not logical: we may feel guilty after
    working long hours at the office because there are dirty
    dishes in the sink or the gutter needs repair. It took years
    of practice to get good at guilt, so it will take a while to
    unlearn it. But it can make a big difference in your energy.

    Avoid unproductive and unnecessary habits such as wor-
    ry or nagging. Georgia Ulrich, a creative octogenarian and
    researcher who practices Energy Engineering strategies,
    shares this wisdom: "I find that many problems solve them-

selves while I work at other tasks. When I hit a snag, usually late in the afternoon, I leave it overnight. The next morning, when I am fresh, it works itself out easily. This saying makes the pressure more fun: 'Miracles we do instantly. The impossible takes a little longer.'"

Another good example of blocking unnecessary energy loss would be to find ways of coping with inevitable energy drains such as traffic. Most of us are usually in traffic at least twice a day. So why lose energy over it? Use the techniques described in Chapter 6 to make your time in traffic a plus rather than a minus. By planning ahead and rethinking your attitude choices, you may discover that it is easy to relax in traffic and enjoy using the extra time to plan your day or count your blessings.

3. **Balance by linking.** Add an energy gain to an energy drain, or wear something you particularly like on a day when you face tasks that drain your energy. Here are other examples.

Get help from a person you enjoy on a task that drains your energy. Plan trade-outs with people of opposite hemisphere dominance. You can learn from their work style; they may also find that you can be an asset to them.

Add color and unusual tools to routine paper tasks. In our office we use colored file folders; large, unusual paper clips; and an oversized, well-designed solar calculator to help us to enjoy the routine paperwork. These items not only make the work more fun but help us retrieve things by appealing to the right hemisphere (which is more visual than the left). A real problem can be keeping up with many projects in motion. When we take files out to work on them, we put them inside a certain-colored file folder for the time being. This makes it easy to locate the yellow or orange file, rather than trying to locate the "Time Management" file from several hundred identical manila folders.

If a project is urgent (meaning that it must go out today), we put it in a red file folder. Everyone in the office knows not to put anything on top of red folders so they

ACTION ITEM

Teach the four steps to new energy to someone you care about. Then each of you plan your own way to put them to work for yourself. You might use "choice accountability," in which you each choose to make yourself acountable to the other in a week (you set the time) to tell the other what you tried and how it is working. One important tip here: no nagging. Let the process be one of inspiring and encouraging each other by being a positive role model. Let this be a free choice. If you are gaining more positive, productive, enjoyable energy on a daily basis, it will be obvious and motivating to most of the people around you.

You might want to challenge yourself with the following:

Can you live _____ percent (fill in the blank) of the time at 90 percent energy or above?

Set your goal just above where you are now and continue to increase it as you learn new ways to make progress. Slow, steady progress is usually much longer-lasting than abrupt, giant steps.

won't get buried and forgotten. Our team is conditioned to check around for any red folders to be sure that essential work is done and mailed before quitting time.

4. **Build energy by looking for new opportunities to tuck energy pluses into your day.** The secret here is not to wait until your energy is completely exhausted to do something about it. Frequently renewing and building your energy in small doses is like topping off your gas tank. You can make a quick phone call to a friend or mate to plan a place to meet for a romantic dinner. You might trade out a neck rub with a work partner, take a brisk walk, or run up the stairs two at a time to get the toxins out of your system. Or you could totally relax for five minutes with your eyes closed, taking yourself via fantasy to a refreshing place you would love to be.

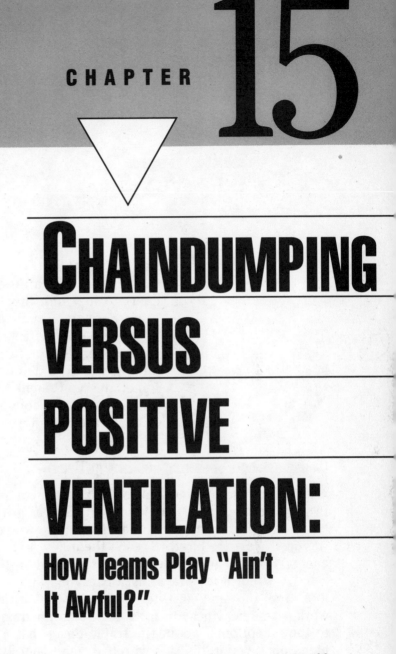

CHAPTER 15

CHAINDUMPING VERSUS POSITIVE VENTILATION:

How Teams Play "Ain't It Awful?"

66 People spend most of their lives worrying about things that never happen. 99

—Molière

66 The problem isn't the problem—the problem is the attitude about the problem. 99

—Kelly Young, age 19

185

Just as certain individuals can exude a positive attitude and high energy, other individuals can drain your energy. Have you noticed yourself suddenly feeling pessimistic, depressed, or fatigued after talking with a particular person? Sometimes you might feel this way in the midst of the conversation and wish to cut the talk short.

Chaindumping—A Contagious Energy Drain

A few years ago we were called in to help a company in trouble. The energy, morale, and motivation of the group was really at the bottom, and their financial picture was moving that way fast! We were hired to teach them how to increase their energy. But first we needed a clearer picture of the problem.

We spent a few days just observing, and one behavior looked all too familiar. One fellow we will call Greg came to work with a heaviness to his walk. He stopped and grumbled to the receptionist about the traffic delay that morning, the high pollen count, his kids who had "made him late," and his car that was requiring repeated service. As he slowly moved on down the hall, the receptionist looked a bit more tired and her voice sounded heavy as she answered the next call.

Greg next stopped in to retell his tale of woe to an associate, only this time the traffic delay was five minutes longer and his car required four rather than three return trips to get the transmission fixed! At midmorning Greg was in the coffee room retelling his litany of woe. His voice was heavy and his posture slumped.

By day's end, we had overheard Greg dumping his problems on six occasions. Each time, his stories became worse as he would feel more and more the victim of these "unlucky" circumstances. We began to notice the contagious nature of the process as well. Others became echoes of him, dumping their own tale of woe on first one person, then another.

In an effort to help this group gain insights into some of their energy drains and discover options for taking charge of their situation in positive ways, we named this behavior pattern *chaindumping*—that is, dumping your problems on first one person and then the next. These are the symptoms:

1. **The same complaints are unloaded again and again.**
2. **The person telling the story is always the victim.** This is the *victim mentality*, when a person becomes the victim of everything: job, spouse, weather, traffic, and so on.
3. **Exaggeration is used.** Details grow and get worse with each retelling.
4. **The problems are dumped on anyone who will listen.** One airing of the bad feelings is never enough.
5. **There is low or no awareness of other choices.** The person does not consider ways to become proactive, plan ahead, or turn negatives into positives.
6. **There is low or no energy.** You can frequently hear a whine in the voice or heavy sighs and groans.

We can all probably think of times when we were champion chaindumpers. At least I can. When I went through a divorce, I must have worn out all my friends retelling my sad story, laying the blame elsewhere and putting my energy into feeling sorry for myself. It was not until much later that I was able to let go of the anger and blame. Only then could I begin to learn how I had contributed to my problems and to discover many positive options for opening my relationships to healthier and happier outcomes.

Think of a very long gash on your arm that must be sewn up with thirty-eight stitches. What if you went around reopening the wound to show each friend how bad the gash was? Each time, the scar tissue would build and the wound would take longer to heal. Nothing would be gained and your chances of healthy healing would grow less and less through this process.

This is a good metaphor for our emotional life as well. Our subconscious doesn't know the difference between a real event and the emotional reliving of an event through remembering or retelling it. Each time you emotionally go back through an incident, it is like having the event happen one more time. And if you position yourself as a helpless victim with no power to change the outcome, you convince your subconscious again and again that it has no other choices.

On the other hand, this is why positive reframing of a negative experience is so effective. If we rethink the experience as we would like it to have happened, we are then rehearsing and practicing other options for the future. The next time we find ourselves in a similar situation, we will have these positive, proactive behaviors rehearsed and ready like familiar friends.

It's easy to see that chaindumping is unhealthy both for the dumper and for the listener. So why do we do it?

The Victim Mentality

If you listen carefully, you will often find evidence of low self-esteem sprinkled throughout the stories you hear. Victim behavior and a feeling of being overwhelmed are two other patterns that are often present. One way to better understand these negative behavior patterns is through a concept developed by Stephen B. Karpman, which explains the dynamics of the roles in a relationship in terms of a triangle composed of Persecutor, Rescuer, and Victim.

When you establish a relationship, you can assume any of these three roles, but regardless of which role you take initially, you will eventually take on all three. Let me explain through my own out-of-balance habits.

At first, I am most likely to be a Rescuer. Here's a typical scenario from my past. If Sue is piled high with work and moan-

ing that she will never get caught up and has to get a proposal out before going home, I might volunteer to stay late and help her (Rescuer role). This becomes a rescue when I take on her problems as my own (as a Victim), not seeing other alternatives for her or for myself. Perhaps in my eagerness to help her, I forget that I have promised my son that I will attend his soccer game and my husband that I will meet him there as well. When I finally leave work and remember my forgotten promises, I rush to the soccer game, already late, and very likely begin to blame Sue on the way. Then as I arrive at the game I may be filled with blame (Persecutor role) toward her. It is now all her fault that I had to stay late (Victim role). I couldn't just leave and risk losing the client. (Remember that I originally volunteered to stay late and help.)

You can see this pattern in parents racing around (rescuing) on Sunday night to help their kids find supplies for science projects that they must hand in on Monday, but that the kids remembered only late on Sunday evening (Victim). Or maybe a father volunteers to coach a daughter's basketball team and then blames the other parents for not helping (Persecutor).

On the other hand, if you prefer the Victim role, it is safer and easier to let others rescue you than to figure out problems on your own. Then if something doesn't work out, it is all their fault. And you can not only feel sorry for yourself for having the problem but also for having to deal with someone who louses up the solution.

If we rescue our children, spouse, friends, and colleagues rather than teaching them to take responsibility for themselves, then we become their victims, being called upon again and again to bail them out. On the other hand, if we learn to ask for what we want in advance and to firmly but politely insist that people treat us fairly, it's amazing what good things can follow.

Life became far more pleasurable and successful when I began to put my energy and imagination into exploring positive ways to invite others to meet me halfway in solving problems. This process helps us understand that we are teaching the people around us how we want to be treated by our actions and reactions. We can choose to take charge of our lives proactively and give up our victim mentality.

Chaindumping—An Expensive Addiction

We're not sure it is scientifically accurate to label chaindumping as an addiction, but as we observe it in ourselves and others, it seems to fit the definition: to give oneself habitually or compulsively to something. Chaindumping is contagious, and once it gets going, it seems to grow. If parents come home chaindumping, the kids will quickly learn to blame their problems on teachers, friends, their poor eyesight, or their siblings—it's easy to find someone or something to blame rather than looking to themselves for the causes and solutions to their problems. If the boss blames upper management, other departments, slow mail, or difficult clients, soon other workers learn that the game is to blame others before they blame you. In fact, people waste lots of energy documenting their actions with paper trails so they can't be blamed.

Victims seek out other victims to help them feel justified in their points of view. They avoid dumping on those who might hold them accountable.

By now you see how we can get on a roll, going through our day dumping negative feelings and stories on innocent friends, family, and fellow workers as we contaminate our day and drain energy needlessly. But don't we all have times when we need to dump and grumble?

There are two points to notice in discovering new perspectives for solving this problem. First, you always have the choice of giving away your power and becoming a victim of circumstance or of proactively seeking ways to affect your situation. There is no freedom without responsibility. When you begin to look for ways to take responsibility, you not only will begin to discover more and more positive options but very likely will experience new energy. Viktor Frankl, who was a prisoner of the Nazis for four years, teaches us that even in the most severe circumstances, the final freedom is the freedom to choose our attitude. "No one can harm me without my permission. They can harm my body but they cannot harm me. I have control of that," Frankl declared. His insights teach us the enormous potential of becoming proactive and self-directed, not even blaming ourselves, but instead seeking positive options and ways we can bring them into being.

Second, when you need to let off steam about a situation, you can ventilate (express negative feelings) positively, in ways that are responsible and not harmful to others. Here are some tips on that process.

Tips for Positive Ventilation

1. **Know when you need to ventilate** (let out negative feelings).

2. **Choose your listener wisely.** This is a time when you will be most tempted to complain to a listener who will side with you and against the other party. Be fair about this. For example, don't ventilate to your children about your

spouse. They can't be objective, and putting them in a position of taking sides is unfair. Neither is it fair to ventilate about the company or your boss to new employees. They don't have the history with the company to know whether you are speaking from facts or feelings, and typically when we ventilate, it is our feelings speaking.

3. **Warn your listener that you wish to ventilate and ask permission before doing so. Set a time limit in advance.** This person may not be able to listen to your problems just now. He or she may be in emotional overload with the situation as it is. Typically we might say, "Got a minute?" This can be a trap because we usually just get started in the first minute; the whole story may take far longer. Instead it is better to say, "I'm hurting and need a safe listener. Do you have ten minutes to listen to my frustration? Then I promise to shift gears." So here is the next step.

4. **Pour out your feelings.** This isn't about logic or who's right. You might remind your listener that you don't want solutions or advice, just support for your feelings even if they are out of bounds. Since your purpose is to ventilate negative or pent-up feelings, really get them out. The goal is to get all the emotional turmoil expressed so that the vulnerable little kid of your right brain gets affirmed and heard in the process.

5. **Now either shift into a problem-solving mode or balance by giving equal emphasis to positive communication and thoughts.** Notice that the left brain joins the right brain in this. Chaindumping is "half-brained"; positive ventilation is whole-brained.

I learned this lesson from my husband, Larry. Early in our marriage when he would come home from work, I would be filled with complaints about contractors remodeling the house and problems with the kids. He would invite me to get my running shoes. To get him to listen I would have to keep up with him. The more I complained, the brisker his pace became. I learned to grumble quickly because I didn't have his stamina, and I sure wanted him to hear me.

One evening when I was particularly filled with woe, I stopped my sad saga just long enough to ask when we were going to turn around and start home. "As soon as you have finished airing problems," he said with patience that let me know he could walk on for hours. I was ready to turn around right then, so I announced that I was through complaining. We turned toward home but after walking a few blocks, I remembered a few more complaints. Without saying a word, Larry turned the other way. I got the message quickly.

I don't want to paint a picture of Larry as being an unsympathetic listener, for that would be unfair. What I learned is that it is far more constructive to sort through problems when you are both walking briskly. The aerobic exercise helps me process more objectively and creatively so that my thoughts are less likely to get blocked by emotional dead ends. By balancing the time spent on problems with an equal amount of renewing silence or cheerful conversation on the walk home, we experience a healing bond. I would encourage you to find your own way to balance negatives with positives.

Protecting Yourself from Chaindumping and Other Negative Behavior

"If you want to change others, change yourself first." We don't know whom to credit for this quote, but it is one that continues to inspire and help us as well as to protect others from our overzealous attempts to change them. We enjoy working on a team where we all strive to practice these ideas, and we are aware daily of how others' good habits help us change for the better. Far more effective than criticism is the role model of positive options. Here are some other tips we find helpful in protecting ourselves from negativity:

1. **Raise awareness.** Invite your closest associates and family members to learn about chaindumping and the positive alternatives. You might describe a behavior you want to change and the ways you plan to work on it. Then ask your listener to help by encouraging any positive changes and gently reminding you if he or she sees you falling back into old comfortable, negative habits. When I expose my own less-than-admirable behavior, this confession seems to free others to admit that they too might benefit from similar changes. The process is as contagious as is negative behavior, but the energy reverses as positive change brings positive energy increases.

2. **Have fun.** Use humor, but be gentle. Unfortunately, most American humor is built on put-downs and negatives. Sometimes it is hard for us to see ways to be funny without discounting ourselves or others. But put-downs to ourself or others cause the vulnerable right hemisphere of our creative little-kid self to wither or withdraw. Be sure to laugh *with* others and yourself, not *at* them. And if you catch yourself being negative and sarcastic with your humor, a sincere and genuine apology can make all the difference. This may take some practice, but it's

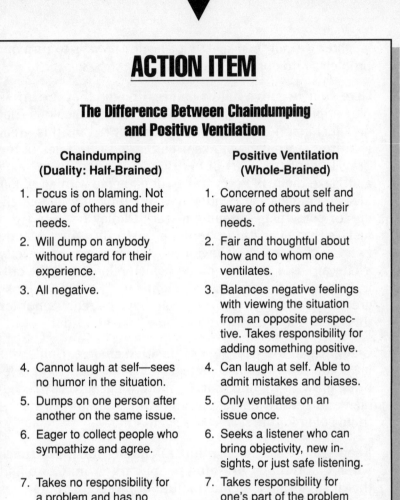

ACTION ITEM

The Difference Between Chaindumping and Positive Ventilation

Chaindumping (Duality: Half-Brained)	Positive Ventilation (Whole-Brained)
1. Focus is on blaming. Not aware of others and their needs.	1. Concerned about self and aware of others and their needs.
2. Will dump on anybody without regard for their experience.	2. Fair and thoughtful about how and to whom one ventilates.
3. All negative.	3. Balances negative feelings with viewing the situation from an opposite perspective. Takes responsibility for adding something positive.
4. Cannot laugh at self—sees no humor in the situation.	4. Can laugh at self. Able to admit mistakes and biases.
5. Dumps on one person after another on the same issue.	5. Only ventilates on an issue once.
6. Eager to collect people who sympathize and agree.	6. Seeks a listener who can bring objectivity, new insights, or just safe listening.
7. Takes no responsibility for a problem and has no intentions of working toward a solution. Believes only others need to change.	7. Takes responsibility for one's part of the problem and makes changes needed for healthy growth.

worth it. Humor is a great way to build energy and relieve stress. It also stimulates creativity and innovation.

During our workshops, audiences laugh the most when we reveal mistakes we have made that remind them painfully of themselves. If it is safe to laugh with us, then it is safe to laugh with themselves. And out of this healthy laughter we can then search for healthier ways to turn our problems into opportunities.

3. **Give your negative habits names.** Pretend they are invisible people, then have fun laughing at their ridiculous (but familiar) solutions to problems. We picked up this great idea from a woman who kept us regaled with tales of the Travel Agent (the part of her that is going to leave home and make them all sorry if they don't agree with all of her ideas!), Priscilla Pig (who solves any difficulty by searching for something fattening to eat), Dudley DooRite (who insists that everything be done perfectly), Aunt Maude (who criticizes her behavior and dress if it isn't strictly Victorian), and the Committee (which refers to all the critical voices in her head). She might say, "The report looks great as is. Dudley DooRite would have us redo it, but for this client and our current deadline, let's go with it."

4. **Celebrate at the first sign of positive change.** Don't wait until you or others are perfect to acknowledge and celebrate growth. We find that the more we generously recognize and reward change and growth, the more we keep them going for ourselves and each other.

5. **Keep your "emotional raincoat" handy for those times when emotionally draining people are around.** We find that just getting a mental picture of protecting ourselves with imaginary foul-weather gear helps us remember to make the mental shift and not lose energy unnecessarily.

6. **Collect positive people.** Plan ways to spend more time with them. Their energy, enthusiasm, and behaviors are contagious.

7. **Look for mentors.** These people can coach you on ways to stay proactive and positive. Ask for and practice their tips and insights.

Bob Gary, an executive at TU Electric, tells how he surrounds himself with positive people:

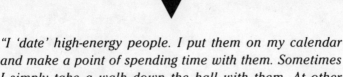

"I 'date' high-energy people. I put them on my calendar and make a point of spending time with them. Sometimes I simply take a walk down the hall with them. At other times, I try to 'hook onto their energy' when I know they are celebrating some kind of success. For instance, I will call to congratulate a guy who is having his twenty-fifth anniversary with the company, because being with high-energy people gives me an energy break in and of itself. I have to deal with low-energy people, too, in my job. I have found the best thing is to challenge those who have a basketful of woes to take time off in order to feel better about themselves. Sometimes I team them up with high-energy people to give them an energy boost and make them feel a part of our team."

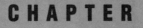
DESIGNING AN ENERGY ENVIRONMENT:

A Nest for Innovation

> 66 *I didn't ever want to have an office, I wanted to have a nest. And it's gotta be packed 'round with the images of all the things I've loved, so I'm totally comfortable in there. A giant nest. I always promise to clean it up someday, but it hasn't been cleaned in years because I've got things on the floor everywhere.* 99
>
> **—Ray Bradbury, science fiction writer**

> 66 *Nobody can be exactly like me. Sometimes even I have trouble doing it.* 99
>
> **—Tallulah Bankhead**

In Chapter 7 you learned the many benefits of adopting a work style that supports your brain dominance. The same factors hold true for your work environment. Think of it as the physical domain in which your mind must operate and your psyche must dwell. Like your work style, your office's structure, ambiance, and organizational set-up can enhance your personal energy or detract from it.

Brain Dominance and the Work Environment

In a set of interviews that Marilee Zdenek conducted for her book *The Right-Brain Experience,* a variety of creative people were asked, "What do you find stimulates your creativity?" "My nest" was one of the responses. Our studies also validate the power of having comfortable and dynamic surroundings. But again, what feels right to one person won't necessarily accommodate the next. To test this premise, just walk past a row of private offices in a large office complex and witness the huge diversity of office decors and styles.

Some desks will be almost bare with just one neat stack of papers centered in the middle and an appointment calendar off to the side. All pens, paper clips, tape, scissors, and other assorted supplies will be arranged neatly in drawers. The walls will have few decorations—possibly a framed degree and professional certificates, a photo of the employee shaking the hand of some government official, and a small picture. But in the office right next door, the desk might be covered with papers, supplies, coffee cups, pen holders, paperweights, books, and framed photos of the family. The walls will display an assortment of items, too—a crowded bulletin board, a large calendar, prints, plants, and overflowing bookshelves. Chances are, if the occupants of the "neat" and the "cluttered" offices were forced to switch desks and work styles for a week, both would be pulling out their hair in two days.

By now you know enough about hemisphericity and its influence on personal work styles to identify which brain dominance belongs to each office. In addition, you can probably cite many reasons why a right-brained employee might feel restricted and uninspired by the first office, and why a left-brained employee might feel disorganized and "crazy" working amid the chaos in the second office. The third important point to understand, both as a manager of other employees and as a manager of your own work style, is that this dichotomy does exist, to the benefit of both types of workers.

Managers and office policies that encourage individual expression in each employee's work site enhance employee morale and energy levels. Unfortunately, the Industrial Revolution fostered an "egg carton" mentality that carefully divided life into separated times for work and play. Standardized methods of production and a heavy emphasis on conforming to the standard were also introduced. This emphasis on standardization affected our business environments, too. We moved into a time of sterile, basic work spaces devoid of anything reflecting the person employed there.

Among the business trends we have witnessed in the past twenty years is the less-is-more, all-business style of office design where family photos (and any other personal aspect of one's life) and informal decorative items were typecast as unprofessional. These items were also thought to be distractions from the work at hand. Another idea promoted by many time management courses was to keep the desk perfectly clear of everything but the one folder of information needed at the moment. A disorganized-looking work space was considered an indication of a disorganized mind.

The latest office decorating trends have let up on this idea, allowing much more freedom for each employee to decorate and organize his or her own space. Without even counting the energy factor, the fact that most people spend more continuous time in their work space than in any room in their house underlies the importance of the work setting.

Making Your Office a "Nest"

Another way to look at your office is as your home away from home. The more personalized and comfortable it can be, the more you will enjoy living in it. It is truly your "nest."

Science fiction author Ray Bradbury is reported to sit amid a collection of memorabilia much like that in the inner sanctum of the Smithsonian. In an interview he noted that he prefers his phone messages to be left in the pattern in which they fall, much like "fallen leaves." He added that it distresses him to have some well-meaning person come by and "straighten them up into a singular, uninteresting pile."

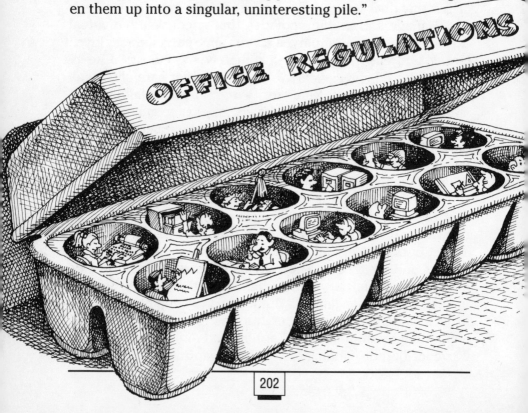

We are stressing the much-maligned messy desk first because it is this style that often needs defending. Have you ever worked with a group that made fun of someone because of the disheveled state of his or her office? If people understand that there is true "method in the madness"—a hidden order within the clutter—then their jokes are not hurtful. But we have witnessed cases in which the state of a person's office made him or her truly suspect by the more conventional people among the group. As you learned when reading about duality, this response is a typical "if-it's-different-from-me-it-must-be-wrong" attitude.

The truth is that many of our most famous geniuses, including Edison, Mead, Darwin, Einstein, and Picasso, have surrounded themselves with work clutter. One of our favorite sayings is "Clutter is the sawdust of a busy mind." A cluttered desk usually indicates that the person thrives on visual order, jumping back and forth from project to project and enjoying the stimulus of seeing his or her work in progress. Furthermore, in most cases the person is aware of the exact location of each item amid the clutter.

As for my own office, I seem to crave and create clutter as a predecessor as well as a product of my creative work. And I seem to need the stimulation of lots of materials and textures around me in order to get the creative juices flowing. I collect old photographs, toys, objects that interest and amaze me, cards and letters that convey warmth and strength, and office equipment and supplies that give me an energy lift when I use them.

The belief that environment can actually be a catalyst for creative thinking is shared by many artists. In an *Architectural Digest* article, novelist John Fowles says this about the relationship between his work space and his own creative dynamics: "Good novels are like good wild plants; they grow out of dirt, the mess of the earth as it is, not as it should be. Almost anything preplanned or decided before a novel is written is potential death to it. The enterprise depends to an enormous degree on sheer luck, and such luck simply does not flourish in the closed universes of immaculate order."

In our organization, Duane needs a minimalist work space in order to be creative. He relates:

"I can't think clearly when my in-basket is overflowing, books and reports are stacked high, and too many supplies are cluttering my desk. If I don't have time to deal with the mess, I will go to an empty conference table to work or simply clear the top of my desk by putting everything in a stack or in a box. But the most important thing is to have a large, clean surface with one ruled pad and a black pen if you are asking me to create something new."

Barbara's office is a blend of right- and left-brained preferences:

"I need both neatness and clutter (visual contact with my work in progress) at different times and stages of my work. Since most of my writing projects involve lots of references and materials, my large desk is scattered with papers and books by midmorning. In addition, I work on five or more different projects in an average week, plus five other projects that are on the "back burner" constantly, waiting for me to make time for them. I need all of them to literally be in view and within arm's reach of me, or else I feel a kind of nervousness, as if I have abandoned them or might forget them. I could not understand this reaction until I took Ann's seminar and discovered my right-brained need for visual references.

But if things get too messy, that frustrates me as well. So on the other side of the coin, I have some strong left-brained needs, such as wanting my environment to look soothing and neat. And when office clutter builds up, I begin to feel irritated. In fact, at times I feel that I can't settle down to work until I have restored beauty to my office and have cleaned up the dishes, newspapers, etc., left in the kitchen and dining area from breakfast."

Personalized Work Spaces
Boost Business

Here's another environment story about an entire company that opted to personalize its setting rather than stick with a bland, conventional office decor. Some years ago our team was hired by a financial institution that was having a problem with employees' low morale. This was during a time when the savings and loan companies in the country were first experiencing a sagging economy, and we were asked to try to boost morale and increase motivation within the work group. Upon visiting the newly built corporate office, we first discovered that all of the staff were required to wear matching uniforms of sorts. Each office looked a lot like the next. Only one piece of art, chosen by the architect, hung in each office. The environment reflected the corporate taste but not that of the people who spent nine hours there each day.

Our first suggestion was that everybody go shopping for a "toy"—something they wanted but didn't need. There was a limit of ten dollars so that each person would feel comfortable with the assignment. They were to bring their item into their work space and note whether the toy made any difference in the way they were feeling. Among the toys selected were a yo-yo, a crystal prism, a bag of marbles, a windup jumping frog, a kite, a tiny teddy bear, a book of poems, and a game of Fiddlesticks. Before long, people were getting acquainted with a new side of each other by viewing and playing with the toys. Initially there was some nervous laughter, but it soon became genuine joy as people began to discover the power of play. There was a noticeable new energy. The fun of sharing childhood memories of toys, games, and other kinds of play stimulated new topics of conversation and new feelings of warmth. Much of the gloom-and-doom atmosphere lifted. And instead of worrying about slowdowns and other obstacles, the groups began to engage in creative problem solving, challenging themselves with more positive questions, such as "What do we have to offer the changing needs of our society?" and "If the trend is away from savings institutions, how can we change with the times?" In addition, a broader group of employees was invited to join the brainstorming groups.

Next the employees were encouraged either to rediscover a hobby or find a new one to enjoy. After exploring their ideas for a month, they were asked to bring some aspect of their interest to work with them. A trust officer brought wood carvings he had been collecting. Watercolors of favorite fishing spots filled one office; desert plants were added to another. Soon each corner of this formerly cold building began to warm up with the personalities of the people who worked there.

Within six months there were some noticeable changes, changes that encouraged the leadership to celebrate the courage it took for them to risk supporting these seemingly irrelevant ideas. Absenteeism and days out had dropped significantly. Much higher energy and enthusiasm were present in all departments. And the "bottom line" had even improved.

When we began to search for possible explanations, we found several. First, customers waiting to see trust officers commented that they would wait longer to talk with the officer whose office felt most comfortable to them. The offices had one glass wall so customers could see the interior from the waiting area. One man had model airplanes very neatly arranged in wall cases. He attracted the confidence of those customers who also had a need for precision and order.

An officer next door had a collection of antique farm implements on his wall. He even had an old pickle barrel for a stool, and several weathered signs from a grocery store were placed here and there. He attracted folks who felt trust and security from this part of history. He recounted that one fellow who had done business with them for years stopped by to ask about his collection. It turned out that they had grown up not far from each other. In the course of their visit, the fellow decided to shift some of his major investments into their trust department. The officer felt sure that without his collection, the link to their past would never have been made.

Second, without realizing it, we had encouraged the employees to fill their work space with items that expressed each individual's brain dominance. These items were harmonious with their self-image and work style, thus reducing stressors and stimulating extra energy.

After you look at the same picture and chair in the same spot week after week, you fail to notice it very much. It becomes part of the expected pattern of things. At a time when life seems to be changing faster than you might wish, familiar surroundings can give you security and energy. But at other times, they can breed monotony. Thus some people rearrange their furniture from time to time and bring in new pictures, books, and decorative items to stimulate a sense of renewal.

One particularly creative president, Peter Van Nort, did a rather revolutionary about-face with a traditional office:

"My present office setup evolved over a period of twelve years. My first step in moving away from the standard office came when I recognized that I did not like to have discussions with people across a desk. So the initial thing I did was turn my desk to face a wall to make such conversations impossible. Then I created a general seating area in my office, with chairs surrounding a coffee table. I also added a tree to the office and gradually began to bring in personal mementos, things that triggered a reaction or questions from visitors to my office. These included framed finger paintings from a child, a patterned wall hanging, and a model outhouse. Later I

brought in one of my favorite books and laid it on the coffee table. The book has lots of photos with interesting phrases beneath them.

Furthermore, I have never liked sitting down at a desk to do my reading and paperwork, so I replaced my desk with a drafting table where I can stand up and work. In the early 1980s, I also was concerned with sharing stimulating ideas and motivation among my staff and visitors to my office. I added items that would stimulate a conversation and turned all my walls into whiteboard areas for brainstorming. These help me illustrate my ideas as I talk, and I welcome others' using the boards as well. Anyone who walks into my office can immediately tell that it is different and that I am open to fresh ideas. I guess the office has a startling effect on newcomers. It stimulates more informal and less conventional thinking.

Most recently, I have added a collection of toys: a 1946 American Flyer train, a gyroscope, jacks, Silly Putty, finger puppets, and anything else that catches my fancy. Often I notice people fooling with the toys during a meeting —it's a great tension breaker."

If you are a top corporate leader, you may feel very nurtured and energized by your traditional corporate office and easily overlook the message. But look again and rethink with us. When you are at the top, you finally have permission to work in an office rich with leather furniture, beautiful woods, and tasteful art. The view is usually inspiring. You are surrounded by awards, pictures, and mementos of high points in your career. But go five levels down in the corporation and you may find sterile, look-alike cubicles with metal furniture and few or no pictures. Standard phones and calculators are visual reminders that the worker is not special, but one of many. Can you see why you might enjoy coming in early and staying late whereas the average worker might not? If by starving the senses we starve the imagination and deplete the renewal of energy for ourselves and others, doesn't it make sense to empower and encourage our team members to create a nurturing environment for themselves?

Designing a Whole-Brained Office Environment

Brain integration is another angle from which to approach the redesign of your office. Rather than create an area that reflects a heavy right- or left-brained proclivity, why not design elements of your office that will promote whole-brained thinking and behavior? A left-brained person can greatly benefit from having items that will stimulate his or her right brain as well, such as brightly colored folders, paper clips, and tabs. Anything that appeals to a sense of beauty or sense of humor will also engage the right brain, as will memorabilia from childhood, family photos, handmade objects, and anything else that evokes emotion.

On the other hand, a right-brained person can redesign certain aspects of his or her office to increase the ability to stay organized. Some left-brain-oriented items that we use include colored files and folders, clipboards with "to-do" lists and "action items," calendars, and schedules. Visual people find it helps to use large clear-plastic boxes for all the files and research of a project while it is current. With a large label, it can't get misplaced and it's easily portable during the working life of the project. We use several brightly colored clipboards to keep up with working papers that are used by several people and, therefore, easily misplaced. We also keep different briefcases for various clients so they can be packed and ready prior to a trip without confusion.

The best way to get an accurate assessment of your individual energy gains and drains is to observe your response to all aspects of your work space. By simply becoming aware of these reactions, you can discover which aspects of your current environment are working for you and which are working against you. The second step is to bring extra high-energy items into your office or to redecorate.

The list of possible high-energy factors is almost limitless, but the following is a grouping of the major categories:

- personal items included in your work area (photos, artwork, inspirational sayings, humorous and playful items, reminders of past achievements, favorite vacations, indicators of your outside interests);

- overall visual aesthetics (color of walls, carpet, and decorations; style and condition of the furniture; existence of windows and quality of the scenery outside);
- noise level (quiet office versus noise from the rest of the building; music you can or cannot control; noise from equipment);
- furniture (Is it comfortable and effective? Does your chair give you a backache? Does your computer give you eyestrain? Is your typewriter efficient, or would a word processor be more than worth the cost?);
- health factors (air quality, lighting, temperature);
- atmosphere (What other settings does your office currently remind you of? What setting would you find appealing—a library nook? a streamlined high-tech research area? a plant-filled sunroom? a creative workroom?).

Office Environment Research Studies

Duane recently visited a landmark research facility studying a number of these office environment variables. The Environmental Simulation Laboratory (ESL) at the University of California at Irvine is the first full-scale university laboratory for the study of office space. It tests workers' reactions to a multitude of environmental factors. For example, the ESL has blood pressure and pulse-testing equipment so that physiological effects can be measured. Soon it will measure adrenaline levels as well. Researchers have come up with several different

yardsticks of productivity, including performance speed and accuracy. Worker morale and mood are also being examined. Explains director Daniel Stokols, "We want to see how these stress levels correlate with changes in the work environment, such as whether people are put near plants, away from plants, whether they're crowded together in a bull pen or more separated with some privacy. We think that those kinds of alterations of the space of an office can have important effects on physiological arousal and stress."

In the March 1986 issue of *New Age Journal,* Sandy Mac-Donald reported on a six-year study done by the Buffalo Organization for Social and Technological Innovation (BOSTI). BOSTI's research indicated that a better-designed environment can increase employee performance to the financial equivalent of 15 percent of each person's yearly salary. Mac-Donald writes, "After studying six thousand workers in more than one hundred offices nationwide, BOSTI's researchers determined that, with depreciation, employers could invest about $8,000 per professional in work-environment improvements (above and beyond normal operating costs) and still come out ahead."

Not only is it true that worker performance on the job is enhanced by attention to the environment, but the converse is also true. Lack of attention to the environment can lower performance. Jean Stellman, coauthor of *Work Is Dangerous to Your Health,* writes, "Research has shown that at least forty minutes of productive time are lost each day because of poor workplace design."

Another fact that comes up repeatedly in research is that the more people are separated behind closed doors, walls, and other barriers, the poorer communication is. After studying this research, Duane decided to move his work space from a partner's desk we shared on the second floor to an open-area work space shared by four production staff. After trying this arrangement for several months, we decided to make it a permanent change because of the increase in communication that resulted. Working side by side with production staff, Duane was able to catch misunderstandings that came from unclear instructions and misinterpretation.

Permission to "Break the Rules" Energizes Your Environment

As a part of our research, my husband and I have been experimenting with our living spaces at home. We had one of those traditional living rooms with a small grand piano in a lovely bay window surrounded by a blue silk sofa, two formal chairs, and a coffee table. It was elegant and lovely—and rarely used. Our daughter, Cathy, would go there to play the piano, but other than that, it only was used for large parties and for Christmas.

We began to wonder how we could use this space so that it would be more inviting, more energizing. My husband loves music and had played the saxophone and clarinet when he was younger. He decided to buy a used clarinet and enjoy playing again. I bought a used set of drums. We added a large bass fiddle and a synthesizer. An antique armoire now holds music cases, a library of music, and my tap shoes, top hat, and silver wig. In the corner an old wooden pony cart is filled with stuffed animals and dolls. There are several tall captain's chairs to invite guests to join in the fun of singing along or just becoming a lively audience. There is even a tin cup to invite tips for the musicians.

Now about once a week we enjoy an evening of music following an informal dinner. And often at midday someone wanders in to enjoy a few idle moments of making music. At first guests are amazed, amused, and puzzled by this unusual ar-

> 66 Here's a whole-brained practical joke on the world's left-brainers. Keep one drawer of your desk empty and each night stuff (and I do mean stuff) everything from your desk in it—pencils, papers, files, paper clips, coffee mugs, the works. Your desk is immaculate and only you know the truth. The risk: if you are going to be away for a few days, be sure to rinse your coffee cup—a giant spore may take over your office if you're gone long enough. 99
>
> —David A. Wilson
> National Director, Professional Development
> Ernst & Young

rangement of musical instruments, toys, and furniture. But soon they are infected by fun and permission to become a kid again and enjoy the playful part of themselves.

Now this won't be the perfect environment for every home or office. But discovering what will invite joy and generate a new enthusiasm and commitment for your work can be a delightful adventure worth taking. If you fear that others will discount you for breaking the norms of conventional office arrangements, share these energy strategies with them and perhaps they will soon realize that you are on the cutting edge of change, setting the pace for increased energy, productivity, teaming, and innovation in the work place.

ACTION ITEM

The first step in redesigning your work area is to evaluate the energy highs and lows that currently exist under each category. The next step is to spend time fantasizing what your "dream office" might look like. The final step is to reduce the number of energy drains and stress-causing factors in your office while increasing the number of energy stimulants. Making your office a balanced, whole-brained environment that invites you to enjoy your work will also enhance productivity and creative thinking.

CHAPTER 17

IMAGING:

Daydreaming as a Source of Energy

66 *Whether you believe you can or can't, you're right.* 99 — **Henry Ford**

66 *As machines' mastery of information speeds up, we will need to rely on people less for facts and more for imagination.* 99

— **Stanley Davis,** *Future Perfect*

66 *What you can do is limited only by what you can dream.* 99

— **Dick Rutan,** *Voyager* **pilot**

66 *I have often been afraid, but I would not give in to it. I simply acted as though I was not afraid, and presently the fear disappeared.* 99

— **Theodore Roosevelt**

66 *It's a matter of attitude, thinking like a winner.* 99

— **Judy Foster,** *The Mental Athlete*

One of the most powerful, energizing techniques you can apply to your work day is *imaging,* or visualizing. This mental exercise is a well-established practice among Olympic and professional athletes, and it is quickly gaining popularity in the business world as well. Author Tom Peters (*In Search of Excellence, A Passion for Excellence, Thriving on Chaos*) has mentioned forms of imaging in his books, as have Michael Ray and Rochelle Myers, the authors of *Creativity in Business,* and many other business and creativity professionals. Here's how it works.

Suppose you are waking up on a beautiful, sunny Saturday morning. You think about all you will enjoy that day, alone and with your friends, playing golf, planting flowers in the garden, hiking in a state park, or lying in a hammock reading a good novel. You are filled with anticipation and energy as you throw back the covers to start the day.

Now presume that you are waking up on an icy, gray Wednesday. The news tells of accidents piling up on the freeways. You visualize a long, tedious drive to work. You feel tired already, and you slump to the shower in a bellicose mood. At work, you review your schedule, grumbling about your back-to-back meetings and the unfinished report decaying on your desk. Your energy sags even more.

But what if you were to receive a surprise call from your honey inviting you to spend an all-expense-paid weekend at a nearby ski resort? Wouldn't your mood and energy level instantly shift, allowing you to enthusiastically attack all your projects with the knowledge that a wonderful reward was waiting for you in a few days?

For most people, the answer is yes. What you anticipate, or vividly imagine, will directly affect not only your energy but your performance as well. As we stated in Chapter 2, research in psychoneuroimmunology indicates that our brain actually produces chemicals that can either add to or block and drain our energy and our performance. Just as adrenaline gives us an instant boost of energy, so can endorphins and a multitude of other self-induced chemicals affect our physical and mental states. In addition, under negative stress and pressure the brain signals the release of chemicals that block or overactivate the immune system, making us more vulnerable to disease and cloudy thinking. You can take control of this process, however, by becoming aware of and guiding the images you create.

Roger Peterson in *USA Today* has reported: "Skaters, skiers, triathletes, and a host of Olympians tell us each night on television how they visualize their winning performances. It may sound like a snow job, but the sports psychology techniques could make us all winners, if we applied them." During the 1988 summer Olympics, many athletes discussed their use of imaging to mentally rehearse (and, in essence, experience) a perfect dive or a winning race. This technique works because *the brain does not distinguish between a "real" physical experience and an imagined one.*

Gold Medal diver Greg Louganis is an avid believer in the power of imagery. He mentally rehearses each dive forty times with relaxing music prior to a performance. When he prepares for the real dive, he replays the music in his mind, dives to the sound of it, and avoids losing his pacing under pressure.

Calming music is an effective tool to help induce a state of alpha. Alpha is a slowed-down level of brain waves, approximately eight to thirteen waves per second, that relaxes people and "awakens" the subconscious. For best results, imaging should be done in this relaxed alpha state when the human mind is most open to suggestion and most capable of dissolving fatigue.

Imprinting Failure or Success

People have always used imaging—they simply didn't call it that. Imaging is literally the process of daydreaming. As small children, we daydream about what we'd like to do, what we'd rather be doing, and what we will do in the future. Think of Calvin in the comics. He is a master of imaging. Imaging takes different forms for different people. For some people, simply kicking back and staring out the window provides an opportunity to imagine a wished-for scene. Prayer is another way that people image. In prayer, we relax, trust God, and open ourselves to limitless possibilities. It is important that the form you choose for imaging be consistent with your values and beliefs.

Scientists are finding that whether the form of imaging is prayer, meditation, or simply daydreaming, a chemical change occurs in the body. Body chemistry and brain waves change as you relax, release tension, and create visual images in your head. The research shows that these changes actually relate to how you behave after the imaging time is over. There is, in fact, a connection between your thoughts and your behavior.

Regrettably, too many people imprint negative images rather than positive ones. Worry, for example, is a backward sort of imaging. We think of all the awful things that might happen, and our body changes (in this case, for the worse). Not only do worry, dwelling on problems, and stress all change our body chemistry and make us more susceptible to illness, but the vivid pictures of disaster we see in our minds are much more likely to become reality the more we dwell on them. That is why it is important to set aside time to imprint positive images.

Any time you worry about a future event, you are imaging. Remember that imaging is simply reviewing or rehearsing mentally a past or future occurrence or action. Some people do this with words such as "My boss will never approve this" or "I don't know how I'm going to make it through the meeting without losing my temper." Other people focus on mental pictures, such as the image of themselves stuttering and losing their place while giving a speech. Visualizing a negative event invites the brain to imprint the expectation and sight of this event. What results is a method of subconscious programming that may affect its true outcome. Do you practice this kind of backward imaging?

The point is that you already are quite skilled at the art of imaging, even if you use it in a disabling way. If you become aware of negative imaging and choose to replace those negative thoughts with positive ones, you can create an energy gain out of an energy loss.

But before you learn the process of imaging, let us warn you to be patient with yourself and not to worry if you can't block out or replace all your thoughts of fear and guilt right away. It takes lots of practice to become good at it, and imaging fear seems to come more easily to people than visualizing success. The first step is simply to pay more attention to your random thoughts and become aware when you are worrying, then to replace these thoughts with an equally vivid positive expectation. You might ask yourself, "What would it be like if the best possible things happened?"

The Process of Imaging

We recommend a several-step method of imaging, with energy benefits linked to each step. In order to place you in control of the process, we'll expand on each of the steps.

1. **Prepare your body through relaxation.** First, get into a comfortable position. Also, if you want to listen to slow, calming music, turn it on. Then follow this procedure:

   - Stretch, yawn, or shake out any stiffness in your body.

   - Close your eyes, if possible, to give you privacy and block visual interference.

   - Focus on taking long, slow, deep breaths.

   - Allow your body to utterly relax, and put any worries out of your mind. As you breathe slowly and drift into a state of relaxation, your brain waves will move into the alpha field, allowing an integration of your logical self (left brain hemisphere) and your imaginative, emo-

tional self (right hemisphere). Listening to the music will also help you synchronize your brain waves, heartbeat, and breathing into a relaxed, rhythmic flow and slow your brain waves to an alpha level.

- Focus on the process of deep breathing for a few minutes. As you inhale, enjoy the pure, fresh air coming into your lungs. Visualize your blood and your brain becoming oxygen-rich. As you exhale, visualize the toxins of stress and pressure leaving your body along with any fatigue, discomfort, or pain. If you create a visual metaphor for this, such as dark smog or dirt being blown out of a vacuum cleaner, you can increase your brain's response to the process.

  These slow, deep, controlled breaths will synchronize your brain waves to your heartbeat and blood pressure, aligning the brain and body. And by getting yourself in sync mentally and physically, you will have more power over the experience.

2. **Prepare your mind by releasing anxieties.** The next step is to take a mental trip to a favorite place. Visualize the environment in detail—its colors, textures, emotions, tastes, smells, and sounds. Think of the good feelings you had there, the moments of success, love, fun, or spiritual renewal. Really free yourself to be there again. If you wish, you can change any details, such as your age, who you are with, and what happens. You might choose a fantasy rather than reliving an actual experience; make it as rich, pleasant, and supportive as possible.

   When you create vivid images of positive events, you cause your brain to release a cocktail of natural chemicals such as endorphins. And with these brain chemicals come not only new energy but an opening and balancing of your immune system as well.

3. **Imprint scenes of success in your mind.** Now you are ready to plant, or imprint, images of successful performances that will lead to optimum energy. You might start by seeing yourself waking early and enjoying a brisk walk, eating a nutritious breakfast, and having a relaxing commute to the office. Go through your day, visualizing energy-enhancing habits such as taking frequent joy breaks, appreciating yourself and others, defusing stress with humor, and drinking six to eight glasses of water.

   Or you might want to visualize a particular success. If you are studying a new computer program or a foreign language, see yourself enthusiastically learning and utilizing your new skill. If you are preparing a presentation at work, visualize yourself successfully giving the talk. Feel yourself being confident and calm, see your listeners giving you nods of approval, and hear your voice speaking clearly and smoothly. Focus on all the clues and signals that would indicate that you have been highly successful and received with enthusiasm.

4. **Reward yourself with a mental vacation.** We also recommend putting a good balance of play, celebration, and simple enjoyment into your imaging sessions. If you use

imaging only to visualize yourself accomplishing a goal, you give yourself no permission to play and relax. But by including images of yourself relaxing and playing, you will automatically look for ways to bring a healthy balance into your life.

When to Use Imaging

Imaging can be very helpful in changing your mental set. The term "mental set" refers to the attitude you choose to take regarding a certain task or that you experience both immediately before and after the task. It is another, more subtle

---

ACTION ITEM

Run a test on the mental sets operating in your own life. Simply select a task that you usually do not enjoy. Check your mood and attitude just prior to the task. How long does it take to talk yourself into starting the project? How quickly and efficiently do you perform it? Do you find yourself making more mistakes on it compared with other projects? Could attitude possibly be the reason you make more mistakes? Do you find yourself fighting to keep your concentration glued to the task? How do you feel when you've finally finished?

Now compare this mental set with one you have about something you relish doing. Ask yourself the same questions and contrast your two sets of responses. Also compare the different energy output that you experience.

The next time you plan to start an initially undesirable task, try reframing your mental set. Spend a few minutes just before you begin and consider all the positive reasons for doing a quality job. Even if the task is not particularly enjoyable for you, you can maintain an energy-building attitude toward it if you remind yourself of the overall importance of your task to the rest of your team. Or consider what it might indicate if you did not have this task to do. For instance, you may not enjoy creating a prospective budget for a new client. But if you didn't have that new client, you might not have such a respectable sales quota for the month.

---

form of imaging that most people overlook, which also can have an enormous impact on your energy and performance.

If the ideas in the Action Item sound familiar, that's because we also discussed attitude shifts in relation to *dualistic thinking*. There we discussed how forcing yourself to do something you've decided you won't like drains energy and throws your right and left brain hemispheres into opposition. Therefore, practicing visualizing exercises becomes another way of achieving synergy between the two hemispheres.

Here's how Loren V. Sprouse, AVP-engineering, United Telecom, changed a negative mental set using positive visualization:

"I needed to write a lengthy report during a time when I already had a work overload and estimated that it would take several days to complete. I considered asking someone else on my staff to do it for me, but I couldn't figure out how to get the information from my head to someone else's without writing down nearly all the details myself. Rather than begin with the project in this dualistic mind set, I decided to try writing the project in a different way.

First I visualized what the finished report would look like and how it should be organized. I imagined writing down my ideas as if I were being interviewed by someone. I had an 'Aha!' kind of insight about formatting the report in a question-and-answer style, with myself considering what kinds of questions my readers most wanted to know about the issue, and in what order those questions would logically flow. Another important insight I had was to try dictating my thoughts rather than putting them on paper because dictation is easier for me.

I had never imagined being able to dictate a first draft of a policy paper that was this complex. Yet to my amazement I had a respectable first draft after about forty-five minutes. Later, as I read through the typed copy of the report, I was surprised to find that very few revisions were needed. I wondered how many other jobs I might have accomplished in one-half or one-quarter of the usual time using this new method. Since then, I have used the method again with equal success."

ACTION ITEM

As you travel home from work (if you work at home, choose a time toward the end of your work day), spend a few minutes recalling only the positives of your day. Think of the goals you accomplished as well as the healthy habits you practiced, the nice conversation you had with a friend, the compliments you received on a recent project, the new idea you came up with, and so forth.

At first it may be difficult for you to congratulate yourself on the good aspects of the day rather than worrying about problems or disappointments that surfaced. If so, this will show you how unaccustomed you are to revisiting your wins. Yet imaging the positives is a highly effective habit of peak performers. Think of it as a mental dress rehearsal for future performances. Also, remember that your subconscious mind cannot tell the difference between a real experience and a remembered one. So to recall a win is like reliving it again. If your mind insists on thinking about what you did wrong or badly, replay that experience, doing it correctly this time.

After trying the imaging technique described in the above Action Item for a few days, notice how you feel when you arrive home. You will probably feel more deserving of and ready for a restful, pleasant evening, because you will gain inner permission to relax by realizing how much effort has gone toward your work day. You will also pick up energy by reexperiencing your wins for that day.

On the other hand, if you focus on what you didn't get accomplished or what you did poorly that day, you will probably arrive home feeling anxious and undeserving of relaxation. You might try to get caught up by working several hours that evening. But too often when we try this, fatigue and/or resentment impairs our work. And without a chance to unwind and restore our energy reserves, we arrive at work the next day feeling burned out. This imaging exercise is a key step toward granting yourself permission to change your evenings by changing your mental set.

Other Times to Practice Imaging

People go through alpha windows, or natural periods of experiencing alpha brain waves, at least twice each day: once when they awaken and again as they drift off into sleep. What you choose to dwell on during these alpha periods becomes powerfully imprinted in your subconscious because your mind is far more open to suggestion, or imprinting, in alpha than in the normal beta state. For instance, can you recall waking to a particular song on the radio, then, off and on for the rest of the day, continuing to hear that song in your mind? Or you may have awakened from a troubling dream and felt the haunting mood of the dream linger for many hours.

In addition to the exercises suggested in the Action Items, there are other great opportunities for imaging. One is when you wake up at night and are trying to get back to sleep. When that happens, some painful memory may be keeping you awake. If you can gently guide your mind toward a positive image, you can create a good experience out of these wakeful minutes. Positive visualizing will help you fall back to sleep with a beneficial mind set. But even if you stay awake, comfort yourself with the knowledge that research has proved that your body can get the same benefits from positive imaging and relaxing as from sleep.

Another way to take advantage of those wide-awake times at night is to get out of bed and harvest your thoughts. Suppose you wake with your mind racing, focusing on all the things you want to accomplish during the next day or week. If you quietly retire to your study or kitchen table and write down your thoughts as they pour out, you may be able to get two hours' worth of work done in much less time. Simply stay with your thoughts until your mind empties or until you feel ready for sleep again. Usually the process of recording these thoughts will reassure your mind that you will act upon them, and then you will be at peace to sleep again.

Visualizing can also be done at the office. Here are a few personal stories attesting to its effectiveness. Randy Harl, president, Power, Brown & Root, had these comments:

"I've always had a vivid dream for myself, my family, and my team and I've realized that I get tremendous energy from frequently revisiting and expanding on my dreams. I was fascinated to learn the technical explanation for why and how this process brings such momentum and synergy into our lives. Our business team now makes imaging a regular and frequent part of our whole-brained teaming process.

One technique our business team uses is 'future focus.' As a team we look at an issue or project as if it has already happened and image exactly what success looks like, in much the same way a high jumper does before clearing the bar. We often use brainstorming to capture the 'dream' from the perspective of each team member. Once we have created a team dream, we can plan the specific steps we must take to make our dream become a reality. We have used this technique for such diverse issues as successful claims negotiation and the development of a new strategy for our business unit, finding that new paradigm two inches above the high jumper's bar."

Bob Gary, a Texas Utilities executive, describes how he uses imaging:

"One of the most effective times I used imaging to change my mental set and give me positive energy was when I was scheduled to give a sworn deposition for a major lawsuit. I knew it was going to be a potentially intimidating experience because we expected TV cameras, lots of attorneys and reporters, and days of questioning. Besides, I was going to be the first person from my company to testify. I wanted to set a good example, to turn it from a negative to a positive experience for myself and those who would come after me. So I decided to spend a lot of time imaging how I would like to appear and how I wanted the proceedings to go for me.

I visualized playing every question put to me as if it were a major poker hand with high stakes. I would either win or lose the biggest poker game of my life based on

ACTION ITEM

Morning Exercise

Upon waking, gently review your day in sequence, imaging it to be as positive and beneficial as it could possibly be. Imagine fun breaks as well as the healthy life-style habits that you would like to acquire. As you visualize your day, see others responding to you in supportive ways. When we imagine others reacting positively to us, they very often do end up behaving that way. We may not have been aware that our body language and other subconscious forms of communication were contributing to their previously negative reactions to us.

If you have a tendency to fall back to sleep while doing this exercise, try gently getting out of bed. Either sit in a chair or begin your morning routine while you do your imaging. You might even try imaging while you are getting showered and dressed. Breathe deeply during this time, and do not listen to the news or talk to anyone. A tape of alpha-oriented music is also helpful to maintain a relaxing state of mind. In fact, some people report that a warm morning shower is such an excellent setting for their imaging exercise that they call it "doing their morning mantra."

that hand. I also decided to dress up for the occasion, to look my best, project lots of energy, and turn the cameras into a plus. My opponents expected me to be wary of the cameras, but I insisted that we not start until they were in place. That unnerved the other side.

The questioning went on for two weeks. Instead of feeling drained and stressed out, by the end of the third day I was being asked by my opponents and the attorneys where I got all my energy and confidence. I was fifteen years older than they were, but they were bushed at the end of each day. I had fun because I went in there with a positive attitude, and I applied what I know about maintaining energy and a sense of humor. The whole experience was actually an energy gain for me."

In the following case study you will hear how a creative servant/leader used imaging over and over again to help his team create a vision and overcome impossible odds to achieve an impressive success. Notice the many ways in which the problem became an opportunity and positive imaging changed the participants' beliefs, significantly increasing their energy. Notice too that the imaging was brought about through typical business practices done in atypical, creative ways. T. L. Thompson, manager of support services at TU Electric, tells this story:

"In February 1987, we experienced a major fire in one of our power plants. It destroyed all the major electrical components in the unit, which furnish us with supplemental electricity during the peak summer months.

The recovery period for this type of destruction is typically very long. Even if the crews worked overtime, at least nine months would normally be needed for repairs. The problem of rebuilding our plant was compounded by its age, which meant that all the replacement equipment had to be reengineered. Also, half a million wires and cables needed to be hooked up to the new equipment.

We knew that if we did not get the plant on line by mid-July we would have to buy the supplemental power from another company. So we set July 1 as our target date. At our first staff meeting, I wrote 'July 1' on the board and asked each manager to write down the single obstacle that would most likely prevent us from reaching that goal. Most wrote 'engineering,' so I took over that assignment to show my commitment and belief that our objectives were possible. And in the face of doubts by top experts, we decided to go for it.

We selected the members of our recovery team based on several factors: their knowledge of our operation, their ability to supply goods and services, and, most important, their attitude about our potential to achieve our July 1 goal. We ended up hiring five corporations. We sat down with the top people and first got their commitment to do everything in their power to meet our objec-

tives. Some said, 'Well, it's never been done before, but we'll do all we can to get there.'

Another critical step we took when choosing our team was to help each company identify its special 'window of opportunity.' One company wanted to improve its track record; another firm's objective was to move into construction work with us. With our internal team, we started off by discussing both the problems and the opportunities. But we focused more on the benefits that this project could bring us, and I asked the team to list our own windows of opportunity. Their answers included developing the expertise of our personnel, building credibility among personnel, and bettering the relationships among staff, both internally and externally.

But we still had to design a formal plan for putting our objectives and opportunities into real life, so we created teams to brainstorm new and faster ways of accomplishing the job. One novel solution was for the construction personnel to create their schedule by planning backward from the July 1 due date. On the engineering side, we decided that by handpicking top-qualified professionals, we could control our quality and goods and services enough to eliminate 50 percent of the normal review process. We also moved everyone in the design stage to the site of the project rather than having them work from their out-of-town offices, and we put the construction management people in charge of the engineering schedule.

I already had my philosophy on visualization before the fire. I believe that we each image either negatives or positives every day. At first I had to do some of both, because you can't just focus on the roses and not see the weeds. But you can visualize those weeds being removed in a positive fashion, and once you have a vision, you can come up with a 'to-do' list to make it happen. I also realized the potential for a midproject letdown, so I imaged those things that would keep 600 people all working happily at something they believed in.

From a morale-building standpoint, one very positive thing was the creation of a pep-rally atmosphere at

ACTION ITEM
End-of-the-Day Exercise

At the close of the evening, as you are drifting into sleep, guide yourself through a review of the day. Focus on the positive events. If you come to a memory of something you don't feel was your best effort, skip over it. The first step is to enjoy celebrating all your positive experiences. Next, allow your mind to consider any negative events, but this time imagine them as you wish they had happened. This step provides a mental rehearsal for the next time the opportunity presents itself, which may be tomorrow or later in the week.

As you go through this second step, be careful not to be judgmental or to revive whatever harmful emotions you felt during the day. Emotions felt while remembering something add power to the imprinting. So if you think about failing to win a new account, for example, and you let yourself feel self-anger or resentment or a drop in confidence, you have just imprinted an expectation of these emotions and the accompanying behavior.

If you still feel sufficiently awake to proceed to a third step, look into the future and imagine what you would most like to happen for you in one, three, or five years. Be inventive, and have fun with this. You can get enormous energy and drive by creating vivid pictures of your dreams. In fact, depression, which is a dramatic energy blocker, frequently is linked to the inability to imagine good things happening in the future.

the plant. We hung banners saying, 'July or Bust.' And some entrepreneurs designed and sold items such as 'July 1' T-shirts that many employees wore. The enthusiasm was infectious. In fact, the degree of commitment and enthusiasm from our people was probably the most important factor in reaching our goal. By June 1, when most of our equipment and cables were in place, everyone realized that our goal was feasible and the excitement level hit a high.

Although a freak fire in one of the transformers pushed us five days outside our initial goal, we still were *ready for the July 15 energy peak. We considered our record-breaking efforts as a great success. We held congratulatory dinners and did many other things to personally thank everyone for their super efforts.*

The final result is that the plant has run as well as any of our other units, with fewer start-up problems than normally occur. Choosing a team of high-quality people was one reason for our success. But having 600 people working on a project means dealing with the average worker, too. I believe that our above-average performance came from the positive attitudes and enthusiasm that spread through the entire work force."

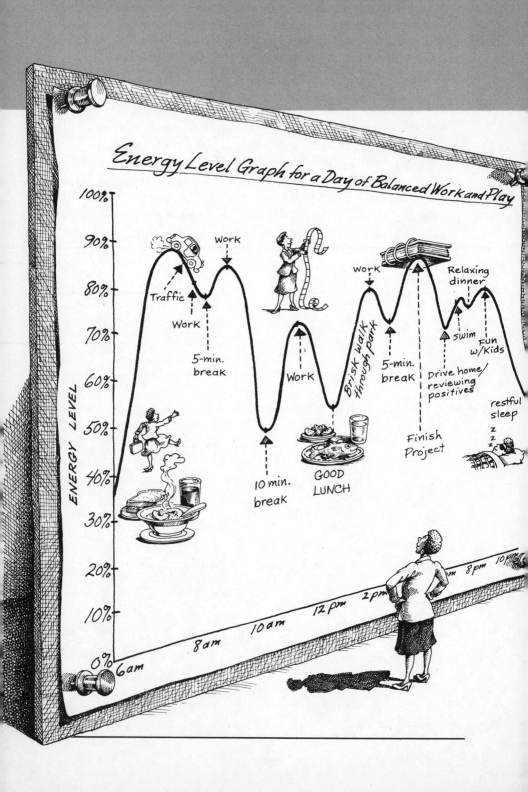

CHAPTER

CHARTING YOUR ENERGY PLAN

❝ *Fatigue makes cowards of us all.* **❞**
—Vince Lombardi

❝ *You only lose energy when life becomes dull in your mind. You don't have to be tired and bored. Get interested in something. Throw yourself into it with abandon.* **❞**
—Norman Vincent Peale

❝ *We love to work because work gives us genuine happiness, the posting and solving of problems, the joyful exercise of the imagination.* **❞**
—Joyce Carol Oates

❝ *About the only difference between stumbling blocks and stepping stones is the way you use them.* **❞**

—Bernard Meltzer, *Bernard Meltzer's Guidance for Living*

his chapter will show you a way to analyze and discover your energy patterns over a typical day and week. The next step is to create ways to infuse positive energy into down times. In our research we noted that high performers consistently gave themselves permission to claim new energy before their current reserves were depleted.

For example, if you enjoy weekends but not your job, the obvious need is to do something to make your job more satisfying and energizing. Changing your work space, adding more appealing tools to work with, taking energy breaks through the day, or going back to school to add skills so you can qualify for a more challenging, enjoyable job are a few strategies to consider.

If you start high on energy on Monday and steadily go down to a low on Friday, you may need some fun to look forward to and renew you through the week. Enjoying a hobby in the evenings, taking a stimulating course at a community college, and sharing aerobic exercise with a friend or mate are a few ways to creatively counter this drain.

The primary goal is to step back and look for the bigger picture in regard to your energy. Over the year you may have high- and low-energy periods. The time of the year when you prepare budgets may take lots of emotional energy and typically cause you to be tense and testy. If you plan ahead and

ACTION ITEM

You may want to quickly chart a profile of your energy level during an average day on the graph below.

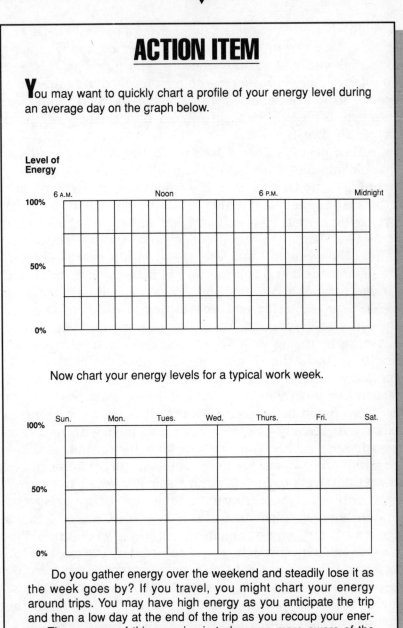

Level of Energy

| | 6 A.M. | Noon | 6 P.M. | Midnight |

100%

50%

0%

Now chart your energy levels for a typical work week.

| | Sun. | Mon. | Tues. | Wed. | Thurs. | Fri. | Sat. |

100%

50%

0%

Do you gather energy over the weekend and steadily lose it as the week goes by? If you travel, you might chart your energy around trips. You may have high energy as you anticipate the trip and then a low day at the end of the trip as you recoup your energy. The purpose of this exercise is to become more aware of the patterns of your energy gains and drains and then to explore ways to move more energy into typically low-energy periods.

enter this period in excellent mental and physical shape and then choose some fun or treats for this period, followed by a wonderful weekend vacation reward, you may find that you can totally change your energy to high levels during this time. You will also have the bonus of a creative, flexible, innovative attitude to bring to your team and of wonderful new solutions to typically draining tasks.

A final idea is to bring your family and/or business team into thinking long term and planning for energy in typically low-energy times. Think of money management as a metaphor. If you just spend your money until it's gone, you have far fewer options than you do if you plan ahead and think of the big picture. The more you practice these creative strategies, the less time you will find you spend in low-energy slumps.

Remember that it is important to listen to your body and respond to what it is telling you. You may need to take a long weekend to just relax and do nothing in order to become renewed. Don't feel guilty about this or think that you should always be bouncing with abundant energy. Rather, seek out balancing states that bring your life the richness that feels right for you. A lazy, relaxed weekend may be wonderful and pleasurable. But this can be very different from landing in a tired, depressed heap after a whirlwind week. It's exciting to discover how many positive choices we have with regard to balancing our energy. The choice is there for each of us!

Study the two energy level graphs in this chapter to see how productive a balanced work/break schedule can be compared with an all-work/burnout schedule. Using breaks as periodic energy replenishers and as rewards for completing a segment of work, you can maintain a good level of productivity and motivation throughout the day. And by the close of the work day, you will not only have enough energy left to enjoy your family and other activities (such as hobbies, reading, or journal writing); you will also feel entitled to a break in the evening because you will feel satisfied with the amount of work you have accomplished that day.

Just the reverse is true when you fall into an exhausting and guilt-ridden all-work spiral. This is how the scenario often goes. Instead of taking a restorative break at 10:00 or

11:00 A.M. when your concentration and interest level start to decline, you admonish yourself and push on. But the longer you work, the lower the quality and quantity of your output. You drink cup after cup of coffee in an attempt to stay alert, but that makes you feel more jittery than invigorated.

By lunch you aren't as far along on your project as you had hoped, so you refuse the offer to go to lunch with your work partners. Finally, you give in to hunger and fatigue at 1:30, but only take time to get a fatty fast-food burger at an outlet around the block. In fifteen minutes you are back to work. Your energy hasn't really been restored because you worried about your work the entire time you were away. Nor has your stress diminished because you ate so fast you couldn't relax. You work through the afternoon feeling tired, distracted, and disgruntled. You have to redo your work several times because of careless errors. You also need to reread many passages since you can't maintain your concentration. And though you are slowly progressing, you feel little satisfaction because you know your work is mediocre at best.

At 4:00 P.M. you call your spouse and say you need to stay late to finish your project. You are reminded of a 7:00 P.M. appointment with your daughter's teacher. Reluctantly you agree to attend, but you insist on staying at work until 6:30. Despite more coffee and a candy bar, your fatigue increases. In the last half hour you barely produce any-thing worth

Energy Level Graph for a Day of Unbalanced Work and Play

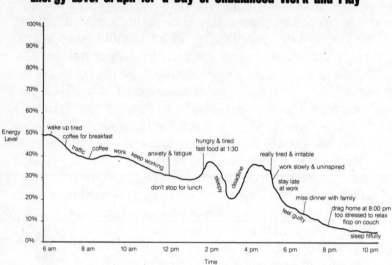

Energy Level Graph for a Day of Balanced Work and Play

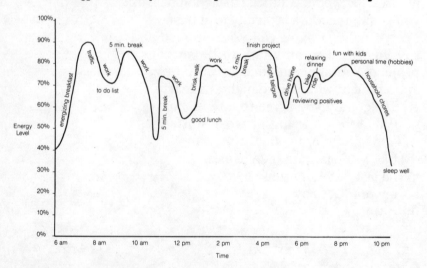

keeping. You are listless and distracted during the meeting with the teacher and you leave feeling guilty.

At home, you are too tired to do anything other than fall asleep on the couch in front of the TV. You haven't done anything to relieve the built-up pressure, though, so you sleep fitfully at night. You arrive at the office the next morning still feeling tired and pressured and lacking confidence, destined to repeat another day of low productivity and high anxiety. Each day gets worse until you fall prey to an illness or mental burnout.

Many of us have fallen victim to this all-work spiral. We have also heard this syndrome referred to as "The harder I work, the farther I fall behind" or "The hurrier I go, the behinder I get." As the chart of balanced work and joy breaks shows, the ninety minutes of idle time each day (a minimum of four five-minute breaks per day plus at least forty-five minutes for lunch) will be more than compensated for by the added energy and productivity you will gain.

We certainly are not the first people to realize the benefits of taking frequent breaks. If you review the profiles of creative people in Chapter 3, you will find that break-taking was an integral aspect of their work styles, too. Schweitzer had his music and gardening to break up his work day. Playful and mischievous, Thomas Edison had impromptu jam sessions with his staff whenever his work became tiresome. He also took frequent motor trips across the country. O'Keeffe liked to begin her mornings and end her days with either gardening or long walks. And Mead devoted her break times to her child, cooking, her parents, and entertaining conversation with her colleagues. Our study of the lives of other geniuses and highly successful business leaders has turned up a similar break-taking pattern in their lives as well.

From our analysis of their work patterns and life-styles, we believe that most of these people had well-balanced, or integrated, brain hemispheres. They intuitively seemed to understand the need for shifting their concentration during the day and for giving their creative, whimsical right brain a chance to surface after intense spells of left-brained thinking.

This chapter concludes with field research results from several of our clients who have discovered the advantages of breaks. Perhaps their examples will provide you with the best verification for the many high-energy benefits of taking breaks both at work and in the evening. Some of these quotes also attest to the value of working according to your brain dominance.

Dave Johnson, quality management and training manager for Brown & Root Power, shares these observations:

"Excitement is a must in our training classes. Students need energy to learn. We at Brown & Root have learned to incorporate color, sound, activity, and lots of breaks in every class to keep interest and energy high and to make learning a joy. In our Crafting Quality classes, student comfort and enjoyment come first, and learning is the dividend."

Ed Platt, a Texas Utilities engineer, tells this story:

"About two years ago I found myself coming home from work totally drained. I had no energy for any activities except my job and family. I had no interest in hobbies and outside activities. At that time I knew nothing of Energy Engineering.

In November 1985, my wife and I went to a stained-glass shop and commissioned a special piece of glass for an anniversary present. The owner told me I should take a class and learn to do glasswork. Over the next two years I made more than seventy-five pieces of stained glass. The amazing thing was that I had time to do this when I had felt that I was so tired I could do nothing else. I found myself working on projects in small blocks of time and having several projects going at the same time. When I came home from work, the glass projects were a release and an energy builder. The handwork let me forget about other cares. The elements of color, texture, and form were not in anything else I did and thus made the work more enjoyable.

I learned a very important lesson as people became interested in my glasswork. Several times I committed myself to projects and schedules rather than just letting it happen at my own speed. It was not nearly as much fun or as energizing. Now when I work on a piece for someone, it is without a schedule. For me, committing to a schedule was contamination of my joy time.

My stained glass hobby has also revived some other hobbies such as photography. Again, I discovered that I can find time and have energy to do things I couldn't do before. It's a thoroughly enjoyable hobby that has had benefits far beyond its cost and that in my mind incorporates many of the Energy Engineering concepts."

John H. Carlson, vice president for Gas Plant Operations, TU Electric, confirms the value of energy breaks:

"I learned as an adolescent to play the piano for my mother. (The lessons were a very left-brained, disciplined experience.) In retrospect, the entire effort was an energy drain and a somewhat frustrating experience. I quit studying and didn't play the piano for about ten years. After college and a family of my own, I discovered how energizing music can be to me and what a wonderful tool it is to build relationships with my children. I had been wanting to learn how to play the guitar and at twenty-seven I taught myself the basics. At thirty-seven I bought a fiddle and an old pump organ. At forty I purchased a mandolin and dulcimer. At forty-two I was given a mountain banjo. I have learned to play all of these with varying degrees of expertise (I don't play any of the instruments very well).

I use these instruments in 'engineering my energy' by playing one or more almost every evening after dinner. I have used a predominantly right-brained approach to learning, 'playing by ear' as opposed to reading music. By selecting an instrument and playing for not more than thirty minutes, I feel more alert and relaxed, ready to spend an evening with my family. Playing music, especially when it is spontaneous and from a right-brained perspective, is very therapeutic and energizing."

SPECIAL ENERGY TIPS FOR WOMEN:

Juggling Work and Home

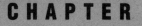

❝ *When we truly care for ourselves, it becomes possible to care far more profoundly about other people. The more alert and sensitive we are to our own needs, the more loving and generous we can be toward others.* ❞

—**Eda LeShan**

❝ *God could not be everywhere and therefore he made mothers.* ❞

—**Jewish proverb**

❝ *Ginger Rogers did everything Fred Astaire did— and she did it backwards and in high heels!* ❞

omen have the same need for a deep purpose to bring meaning to their life as do men. But many of us today are juggling complex scripts that divide and drain our energies. One cultural script says that it ought to be enough to be just a wife and mother, but many of us find ourselves needing other ways to fulfill our purpose. Another script says that if we don't have a career, we are missing out, yet we don't want to sell our marriage or children short. Some of us have aging parents and the related responsibilities. For many, having a demanding job on top of parenting and marriage is a necessity, not a choice. Many more of us are single parents, frantically trying to wear all the hats and juggle all the demands without letting any of the balls hit the floor.

A frequent energy trap for women is needing to please others. Our parents and teachers reward us with their love and admiration when we please them—and withhold it when we dare to please ourselves at the expense of their wishes and demands. It's particularly difficult for a young girl to adopt intrinsic behavior (basing her self-worth on her own standards rather than on those outside her). Our religious institutions, schools, and families typically reward extrinsic behavior (basing self-worth on our ability to meet the expectations, goals, and demands of others). We eagerly become "good girls," "good students," and then "good mothers" by meeting others' expectations. Swimming against the culture is difficult and energy-depleting. Yet until we are able to set our own goals, have our own dreams, and write our own scripts, we are destined to continually feel inadequate because the complex demands of others are at cross-purposes, continually setting us up in no-win situations.

Yet another energy trap is the game of "catch-up" that many of us play so well. We seem to believe that if we can just run faster, compound our efforts, stay up later, and get up earlier, perhaps we can finally get it all done. For me this has been the cruelest illusion. I've become amazingly skilled at getting more and more done in less and less time. But until or unless I learn to step back and reevaluate my expectations, I may never notice that the more I accomplish, the faster the speed of the treadmill of expectations that I and others generate for me.

Creating Options Before You Need Them

In his latest book, *Future Perfect,* Stanley Davis teaches us to think and plan in "beforemath," visualizing events before they happen instead of planning and managing as if the future will be an extension of the past. As we learn to be self-managers, to plan for the long term, and to work more creatively with others in our lives, together we can develop life-enhancing options for all of us.

In the past I tried to do it all alone, responding to one crisis after another, until I finally realized that there just wasn't enough of me left. By observing other creative women, I learned to anticipate needs, and then to brainstorm solutions with the others who were involved. Here are some ideas you might discuss with your employer and co-workers:

- Create a resource bank of child care possibilities for extenuating circumstances such as needing to work late or take extra hours for special occasions, weekends, or trips.

- Explore the possibility of a shared company plan for elder care and encourage a process to create such a program. IBM has an Elder Care Referral Service; at AT&T, employees can place up to $5,000 each year in pretax wages into an account for child or elder care expenses. Stride Rite Corporation has an Intergenerational Day Care Center, which serves the needs of both preschoolers and the elderly.

- Mutually invest in placing a computer terminal in your home, attached to your office by a modem. Then you can easily continue to work at home if a child is ill. Or you might work at home one day a week, saving on child care dollars and parking.

- Think of your career as modular, and create a different pace and phase during the years you want to stay at home. You might take a sabbatical to update your skills. Use this time to read or go back to school, carrying a lighter load so that you can enjoy time with your children while being stimulated by new ideas.

- Help plan and coordinate an evening seminar series on parenting skills. Others who are facing the difficult issues of juggling career and family might be eager to join in the discovery of positive options through coaching with a counselor. We often try to compensate for our lack of time with our children by giving too much financially or promising too much of ourselves instead of planning realistically and calling on children to pitch in and help with family chores or earn their own money to finance their wishes and dreams.

- Suggest a study of job sharing. Are there full-time positions two people might share? What are the benefits and trade-offs for the company, other workers, and participants?

You can see how you might create many more options for everyone in a positive, low-risk atmosphere by exploring possibilities long before the urgent need arises.

Putting First Things First

One of the most important ways we can give to others is to take good care of ourselves. When we always put ourselves last, our energy and our health can suffer and everyone loses with us.

Betty Hudson Bowers, vice president of government relations for Fluor Corporation, in a career that demands long hours, a hectic pace, and lots of travel, makes morning exercise a vital part of her high-energy routine. She says,

"My workout consists of one-half hour of aerobics followed by one-half hour on a rowing machine. By the time I get to work, I'm in full gear, ready for a fast-paced day. The mornings are my own, and I like the feeling of taking care of my personal needs before devoting myself to the needs of the company. On those days when my travel schedule does not allow me to exercise, I truly miss it."

Reciprocity

One of the most valuable tools I have learned is the skill of reciprocity. This means creating ways for both parties to get their needs met. What can my child, my spouse, my parent, my co-worker do for me that will free me to provide the time and energy they need from me and also allow me the time needed for healthy balance in my life?

I relearned this from a graduate student who told about going home from class one day to a bitter evening of crisis with her three school-aged children. As she finally broke down, sobbing, the children gathered around her in great concern. For the first time, she admitted her fears—that as a single mother, trying to provide for them while going back to school to improve her career level, she couldn't get it all done. To her amazement, when the children saw that *she* needed *them*, they willingly pitched in to help. Together, the four of them created a plan with roles for each of them. The older daughter helped the younger children with homework. They took turns packing lunches and shared household chores, and they created money-

saving ways to have fun that took some of the pressure off their mom when she had long work hours.

In the end, the children gained self-esteem as they learned that they each had something to contribute. Their mom gave them not only the precious gift of her love and support, but the gift of learning to become both independent and interdependent.

Give the Gift of Self-Management and Interdependence to Your Family

I have carried a lot of guilt from my years of single parenting and being a working mother while going back to school to earn advanced degrees. The only way I could survive was to insist that my son, Rayo, partner with me in doing everything around the house from cooking to shopping to laundry. I knew that it embarrassed him for his friends to know that he could iron and cook, but I never thought I would see the day when he would actually thank me.

After his first few months away at college, he came home with funny and touching stories that I offer to other guilty moms.

Rayo told of one boy who went to the quick-stop food store to buy milk, eggs, and butter and then stored them in the top of his closet. Rayo said, "The poor guy didn't even know these foods need refrigeration." Another freshman piled his clothes in the corner for days and then seemed puzzled that they had lost their magic. "At home, I piled them up when they got dirty. Next morning they were clean, folded, or hung in my closet. I don't know what's gone wrong." Rayo saw still another classmate bring his dirty clothes down to the laundry room and stare at the machines in bewilderment.

That's when my son told me he actually began to appreciate what I had done. "I used to feel sorry for myself. I didn't realize the gift you were giving me. Most of these guys don't even realize they don't have the skills to become independent. Thanks for loving me enough to prepare me to be on my own and take care of my own needs."

So, moms, when you encourage or insist that your children help you out at home, think of it as doing them a big favor. Sometime in life we all need to take care of ourselves. Better now than later!

Letting Your Mate Be a Help-Mate

The children grow up and leave, but with luck, your husband will be around for a long time. That is why it is essential to enlist his aid in your effort to take good care of yourself.

Many husbands realize that their wives carry an unfair share of the load, but often they have no idea how they can help. The first step is for you to talk about your specific situation with your husband. Then you can brainstorm together to find ways you can help each other to a more satisfying division of labor.

Carolyn Bechtel describes how she and her husband, Gary (president of Bechtel Corporation Civil Company), solve the problems that many executive couples face:

> *"With our livelihood coming from the engineering and construction business, heavy travel, long hours, and frequent moves are a given. All this plus many other stressors can*

make the responsibilities of being a corporate spouse and mother of three young children a big challenge and a potential energy drain. Gary has been great about searching with me for solutions that support all our needs. Here are some of the things that make a big difference for us in keeping our energy and spirits high.

Gary includes me in reflecting on his business role and frequently invites my ideas. As a result, I feel part of things and not left out. He is encouraging his management team to find creative ways to support and respect the needs of the family.

He is open to my feelings and needs and those of the children. Everyone is consulted when we make a move. We work together to create options so everyone feels valued and contributes to helping the others. We all feel as if we help make Bechtel more successful.

Gary's business will be taking him to other parts of the world, which of course means more and longer trips. We are planning on taking our children on some meaningful trips to some of these job locations so that they, too, will be eager to go the second mile with some patience and understanding instead of resenting the heavy demands of company responsibilities.

Probably the most important energy factor is our learning to get all our feelings out on the table honestly without blaming. Honoring everyone's feelings and point of view in searching for mutual solutions is a new skill we are eager to share with our children. When it's safe to make known your feelings, needs, and wants and be in on the big plan, life is far more rewarding and fun."

People Support What They Help to Create

This is a well-known management concept. Getting others to come up with creative solutions to mutual problems is a key step in the right direction.

A business friend was facing surgery at the same time her housekeeper was going to be gone. For six to nine weeks she would be unable to meet her regular family responsibilities. She invited her husband and two teenaged sons to a family meeting, and together they wrote out and posted a list of the essential chores that kept the family running. Then they began to come up with positive solutions.

Her husband volunteered to do the shopping on the way home from work. He also noticed that the dog groomer was near his office and that he could easily take care of this monthly chore. The boys bargained and traded housework chores and suggested TV dinners and take-out food to cut down on cooking and cleaning. They were all amazed at how easy it was to design a whole new system for getting everything done. When my friend's recuperation was completed, not only did the family appreciate her efforts more, but she also had willing helpers on chores that used to be hers alone.

If she had assigned people to jobs, she probably would have battled resistance. But by stating her needs and asking for help, she got her family involved in creating the solution. And in the process, they also took ownership of the solution.

Creative solutions to the energy issues of women need not be limited to women. We can also learn from single fathers. A divorced business colleague had his three school-aged sons visit him for the summer. The first evening after work the boys were eager to see their dad. They went to the pool together, played some tennis, had a fine dinner, enjoyed television, and went to bed.

The next evening, the boys were ready to go to the pool as soon as their dad got home. He lived in an apartment complex where children could only use the pool with an adult along. Their dad apologized and said, "I wish we could all go to the pool. But I have to shop for groceries, cook the dinner, and get some clothes clean for tomorrow. Maybe if you boys could get some of this done before I come home from work, we'd have more time for fun."

To his surprise and delight, that was all it took. The next evening when he got home, his suit and towel were out and ready. The boys had salad all prepared in the fridge. The table was set. They all enjoyed a fine evening.

After that, he planned with them each evening what needed to be done the next day. If they managed to do it, the next evening would focus on shared fun. When they didn't, he simply did the work and left the boys wishing for his companionship. This only happened a few times; the boys were so eager to enjoy time with him, and he got so good at appreciating their efforts and helping them plan, that they had a great summer together. And their mom was delighted at the new skills and spirit of cooperation they brought back with them in September. It was a true win-win-win situation!

Ask for What You Want in Advance

I learned the hard way that you get much more willing cooperation if you ask for what you want in advance, so that others can plan around these requests.

When my two stepchildren were preparing to go off to college for the first time, I was whining to one of my friends that they would probably leave their rooms in an awful mess and I'd get left with the big cleanup. She asked if I had asked for their help. My response was, "Fat chance!"

But, since I teach this stuff, I thought it only fair to give the kids the benefit of the doubt. And I am here to eat humble pie. I said something like, "I know it's a really big job getting everything organized, loaded, and off to school for the first time. It would really mean a lot to me if you would plan to allow enough time to clean your room before you leave home. Perhaps you could leave it the way you would want to find it when you come back."

To my absolute amazement, both kids left their room in fairly good shape. I made sure to write them a thank-you note. That was several years ago, and they have never left their rooms in a mess since. What a nice lesson for me to learn!

When my stepdaughter was a teenager, she could make a simple trip to buy white tennis shoes take hours. I was pushed with my dual schedule so I made a deal with her. She was too young to drive so I was the taxi. I invited her to trade out time with me. If she needed me to drive her for an hour, she could trade any household tasks that she could do in the same amount of time. This time allowance was like a bank account. If she didn't have time in her account, I didn't drive.

As a result, she learned to call ahead, know where she could buy shoes in her size, have the check made out for the amount, and be in and out of the store in a flash. Her shopping became lightning fast and she became much more aware of how her habits affected others.

Energy Tips for Being Single: Learning to Love Yourself

After my divorce, I was single again for eight years before I remarried. I learned many valuable lessons during those difficult years. The most important had to do with how to enjoy time alone.

I couldn't figure out why I dreaded being alone until I stopped one day to reflect. I was always very creative about noticing what others liked and making my time with them special. If they liked classical music, Mexican food, or jogging, I would plan time around their special likes. But when I was alone, I planned nothing.

I began to ask myself: What if I treated any other person the way I treated myself? Notice the ways I discounted myself and sent a strong message that I didn't matter.

1. If I knew I would be home alone, I'd typically work late. Why not? I didn't have anything special planned for later.

2. When I got home, I'd slip into "something comfortable"— so comfortable that if the paperboy came to collect, I'd hide behind the door in shame.

3. I'd usually go to the fridge and graze with the door open. Dinner might be leftovers, eaten from a plastic container. Not even a plate at the table, let alone a placemat and napkin!

4. Later, I'd flip on the TV and drift off to sleep because whatever came on probably wasn't interesting and I was too tired to care, much less change the channel.

5. If anyone called with any other options, even if it was a neighbor asking for help moving a piano, I'd jump at the chance. I was lonely for companionship, but I didn't know how to give it to myself.

Now, imagine you were my guest for the evening and I treated you the way I treated myself: sloppy attire, leftovers eaten while standing at the fridge, staring at "anything" TV, going to sleep from boredom and fatigue, or standing you up for any possible excuse, such as helping a neighbor move. I couldn't be more rude and insulting!

Another telltale symptom was how I responded to invitations. When someone asked where I wanted to go for dinner, I would respond, "Oh, wherever you do." Asked what I wanted to do that evening, I might say, "Whatever pleases you." Or questioned about what movie I wanted to see, I'd probably answer, "Just suit yourself." I was so out of balance trying to please others that I had failed to develop my own desires and opinions and ways to make them known. And in this process I had become a nonperson. No wonder I was terribly lonely when I was alone! There was no one home within me!

That gave me the idea to begin dating myself. Does this sound crazy? Give it a chance.

I would pick one evening a week for my time with me and would plan something really special. I vowed not to break my date with me no matter what else came along, short of a major crisis.

It was awkward at first but soon became fun. I would stop on the way home and buy myself a long-stemmed rose or something special that I loved to eat. I might cook to George Gershwin's "Rhapsody in Blue," eat on a linen placemat in the garden by candlelight, and take a long bubble bath with classical music and a glass of champagne in special crystal. Or I might put on one of those long, lovely dresses I had in my closet but never had occasion to wear to enjoy an evening of entertaining reading.

I actually began to look forward to my evening with me! What a change. I now wonder if I could ever have been a partner in a healthy marriage if I hadn't learned my own worth. Until I valued myself, how could others value me? I now suspect that this has been the most significant change in my self-image and my own emotional health.

How does this attitude affect your energy? When you are having fun or have something to look forward to, you have more energy. When you have positive plans, you work productively and eagerly. When there is only work out in front of you, and more of the same after that gets done, you slow down without realizing it. Your feet and your spirits drag.

So valuing yourself and knowing how to insist that others value, appreciate, and partner with you are significant secrets toward creating a synergistic, interdependent life-style. And that is the key to enjoying abundant energy on a daily basis.

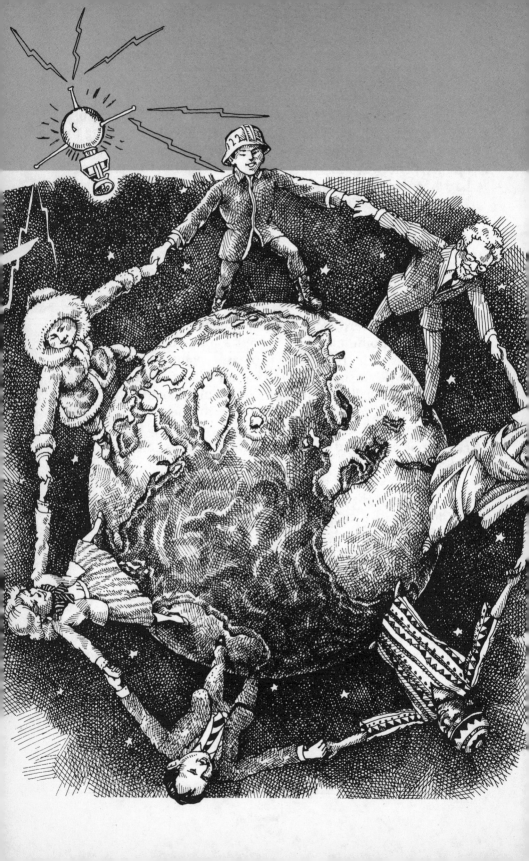

CHAPTER 20

ENERGIZING YOUR PERSONAL POWER AND POTENTIAL:

The Unlimited Growth of Balance

❝ *One person with a belief is equal to the force of ninety-nine.* ❞

—John Stuart Mill

❝ *The best way to predict the future is to invent it.* ❞

—Alan Kay, Fellow, Apple Computer

❝ *I want to be completely used up when I die . . .* ❞

—George Bernard Shaw

❝ *The biggest risk is to do nothing when the world is changing rapidly.* ❞

—Walter B. Wriston,
Retired Chairman, Citicorp

When we are tired, our bodies and brains are filled with toxins that block the effective processing of new ideas. Even if we have a winning plan, when we are exhausted it can seem more like an adversary's plot to keep us on the treadmill than a path to new, innovative successes. We are more likely to duck and avoid risk, new roles, and new ways of thinking. At a time when continuous improvement in performance is essential for each of us in order to move our corporate and family teams forward to greater success and health, a refreshing and dependable source of high-energy strategies and life habits is the key.

It has been seven years since we began our research on personal energy, and so many new insights have built one upon the other. We have learned that there is no ceiling on our energy potential. It is not unusual for clients to estimate personal energy gains and increased productivity at four or five times their entry level (and all participants began as pace-setting leaders in their fields). In addition, there is the network effect. When your partners and peers bring increased energy, innovation, and flexibility to the team, the momentum becomes synergistic. Our clients teach us about energy as we teach them. In each of the past seven years we've significantly increased our productivity, energy level, fun quotient, and balance.

The quest for unlimited energy is a never-ending journey. The more we learn, the more skillful and resourceful we become. When we ask former Perspective III participants what differences Energy Engineering has made in their life, they typically report that they have more fun at work, more joy breaks, more quality time with their family, less pressure and more enthusiasm, more creative solutions to problems, and more positive imaging. And as we interview family and work partners, we hear similar reports of far less pressure, more effective communication, better teaming, more celebrations, better listening, and lots more creative options coming from everyone.

There is a "neural network" in the making as groups of people are learning to be so intuitive to each other's needs and meanings that they often know what is happening without being told. Spouses and other family members are contributing in unique and creative ways to the enrichment of the "corporate family." Family and personal needs are becoming a higher priority in creative, win-win planning. And as a result, corporate goals receive the benefit of the enthusiastic energy of balanced employees supported by healthy families.

Abundant energy can only come by giving up victim behavior and adopting proactive, self-actualized options. Blaming and accusing others is being replaced by enjoying creative problem-solving sessions at home and at work. When people become empowered with a new sense of unlimited personal potential, the energy is contagious and a clear benefit to all. In essence, as more and more people bring balance into their work and life-style, a creative resilience forms a solid foundation that is necessary to support the rapid change taking place across the globe.

As we move toward the year 2000, the pace seems to be quickening and the changes keep coming, faster and faster, even in areas we thought would never change. All around us we hear paradoxical thinking:

"You must slow down to go faster."

"If you want to change others, change yourself first."

"To become a more productive worker, make sure you take time regularly to enjoy refreshing play."

"If you want to increase your success rate, increase your failure rate!"

"To succeed in a competitive global business environment we must learn not only to survive in this chaos of rapid change, but thrive on chaos," warns Tom Peters, author of *Thriving on Chaos*. Information is doubling, maybe even tripling, every decade. Technology is changing so rapidly that all of us must keep learning monthly to just stay current.

In short, the old ways of doing things are no match for the high-energy demands of leading a quality life in today's atmosphere of rapid change. In addition, when we are threatened, we typically shift into a defensive mode and become entrenched in familiar, time-tested, habitual ways of thinking and behaving. With threat and change we are most likely to withdraw into half-brained duality, blaming and accusing those who are not like us.

Yet those who are different from us or strong where we are weak become precisely the personalities who threaten us most. *We need most what we find most threatening.* To find the balance that is so critical to mental and physical well-being and to create the synergy of whole-brained creativity and energy, we need not only to make friends with our opposites but also to become interdependent team players, both with our own shadow side and with those around us who see what we can't and who think in ways that we find threatening.

The rewards of all this upheaval are tremendous! As we learn to change our mental set, recognizing that the freedom to choose our attitude is one key to discovering new energy, problems become opportunities. And as we learn the secret of making paradigm shifts to see the world anew and to make what seemed to be impossible possible, we learn the secret of unlocking new and significant energy.

We are talking about a holistic process. Our brains and bodies are "hard-wired" into each other. As we integrate our two brain hemispheres into a mutually supportive team, we

discover not only that any problem can be an interesting and exciting challenge but that we can even have fun in the process. We find that an abundant energy and enthusiasm results from the enjoyment and satisfaction we get as we make one breakthrough after another. And we learn the deep spiritual joy of servant leadership as we discover that by quietly listening to, supporting, and empowering others, we become more valuable and fulfilled.

One added benefit to whole-brained integration and teaming is the gift of a stronger, more active immune system that leads to more energy and therefore better physical health. We know that long periods of distress or anxiety-producing stress release floods of adrenaline, which block our immune system.

But as we learn to thrive on chaos, to think of problems as opportunities, and to have fun and feel enthusiastic about the unlimited potential of ourself and others, our bodies produce positive chemicals that bring our immune system into balance and thus result in greater health.

The ideas and principles offered in this book invite you to explore givens in your life that you have not previously questioned. Why would you want to challenge your present system? The goal is to shoot an arrow first and then draw the target around it. You're in the bull's-eye every time because you have the answers to questions that haven't been asked. By tapping whole-brained energy and establishing synergistic habits before the crisis hits, you are prepared for the worst and can make it the best.

Your best today is not good enough tomorrow! As everything continues to change and accelerate around us, technology either bombards us or anoints us with multiple opportunities to accomplish everything faster. Can the human brain keep up? This is our challenge, and energy is the key.

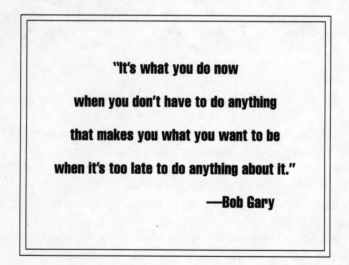

"It's what you do now

when you don't have to do anything

that makes you what you want to be

when it's too late to do anything about it."

—Bob Gary

BIBLIOGRAPHY

Beattie, Melody. *Codependent No More*. New York: Harper & Row, 1987.

Bepko, Claudia, and Jo-Ann Krestan. *Too Good for Her Own Good: Breaking Free from the Burden of Female Responsibility*. New York: Harper & Row, 1990.

Bolles, Richard Nelson. *What Color Is Your Parachute?* Berkeley: Ten Speed Press, 1974.

Capra, Fritjof. *Uncommon Wisdom*. New York: Simon & Schuster, 1988.

Cerf, Christopher, and Victor Navasky. *The Experts Speak*. New York: Pantheon, 1984.

Cousins, Norman. *Anatomy of an Illness*. New York: W. W. Norton, 1979.

Cousins, Norman. *Human Options*. New York: W. W. Norton, 1981.

Covey, Stephen R. *The Seven Habits of Highly Effective People*. New York: Simon & Schuster, 1989.

Davis, Stanley. *Future Perfect: A Startling Vision of the Future We Should Be Managing Now*. New York: Addison-Wesley, 1987.

Dossey, Larry. *Beyond Illness: Discovering the Experience of Health*. Boston: New Science Library, 1984.

Dossey, Larry. *Space, Time and Medicine*. Boston: New Science Library, 1984.

Frankl, Viktor E. *Man's Search for Meaning*. New York: Washington Square Press, 1985.

Garfield, Charles. *Peak Performers: The New Heroes of American Business*. New York: William Morrow, 1986.

Greenleaf, Robert K. *The Servant as Leader*. Indianapolis, Ind.: Robert K. Greenleaf Center, 1991.

Hansel, Tim. *When I Relax I Feel Guilty*. Elgin, Ill.: David C. Cook Publishing, 1983.

Hiebert, Roselyn, and Ray Eldon Hiebert. *Thomas Edison, American Inventor*. New York: Franklin Watts, 1969.

Hoff, Benjamin. *The Tao of Pooh*. New York: E. P. Dutton, 1982.

Houston, Jean, and Robert Masters. *Mind Games: The Guide to Inner Space*. New York: Dorset Press, 1990.

Howard, Jane. *Margaret Mead: A Life*. New York: Fawcett, 1985.

Kenner, Hugh. *Bucky: A Guided Tour of Buckminster Fuller*. New York: William Morrow, 1973.

Kipfer, Barbara Ann. *14,000 Things to Be Happy About*. New York: Workman, 1990.

Levinson, Harry. *Executive Stress: Learn to Overcome the Pressures of Corporate Life*. New York: New American Library, 1975.

Lisle, Laurie. *Portrait of an Artist: A Biography of Georgia O'Keeffe*. Albuquerque: University of New Mexico Press, 1986.

McGee-Cooper, Ann. *Time Management for Unmanageable People*. Dallas: Bowen & Rogers, in press.

Manchester, William. *The Last Lion*. New York: Dell, 1989.

Maslow, Abraham. *The Farther Reaches of Human Nature*. New York: Penguin, 1976.

Maslow, Abraham H. *Motivation and Personality*. New York: Harper & Row, 1970.

May, Rollo. *The Courage to Create*. New York: Bantam, 1975.

Miller, Peter M. *The Hilton Head Executive Stamina Program*. New York: Warner Books, 1988.

Ornstein, Robert. *The Psychology of Consciousness*. New York: Harcourt Brace Jovanovich, 1977.

Payne, Robert. *The Three Worlds of Albert Schweitzer*. Nashville, Tenn.: Thomas Nelson, 1957.

Peters, Tom. *Thriving on Chaos: Handbook for a Management Revolution*. New York: Knopf, 1987.

Peters, Tom, and Nancy K. Austin. *A Passion for Excellence: The Leadership Difference*. New York: Warner Books, 1989.

Peters, Tom, and Robert Waterman. *In Search of Excellence: Lessons from America's Best Run Companies*. New York: Warner Books, 1988.

Porter, Kay, and Judy Foster. *The Mental Athlete*. New York: Ballantine, 1990.

Ray, Michael, and Rochelle Myers. *Creativity in Business*. New York: Doubleday, 1986.

Rifkin, Jeremy. *Time Wars: The Primary Conflict in Human History*. New York: Simon & Schuster, 1989.

Robbins, John. *Diet for a New America: How Your Food Choices Affect Your Health, Happiness and the Future of Life on Earth*. New York: Stillpoint, 1987.

Saint-Exupéry, Antoine de. *The Little Prince*. New York: Harcourt Brace Jovanovich, 1982.

Scott, Dru. *How to Put More Time in Your Life*. New York: Dutton, 1984.

Sher, Barbara, with Annie Gottlieb. *Wishcraft: How to Get What You Really Want*. New York: Ballantine, 1983.

Sperry, Roger. *Science and Moral Priority: Merging Mind, Brain and Human Values*. New York: Praeger, 1984.

Springer, Sally P., and Georg Deutsch. *Left Brain, Right Brain*. New York: W. H. Freeman, 1985.

Stellman, Jeanne, and Susan M. Daum. *Work Is Dangerous to Your Health*. New York: Random House, 1973.

Tolkien, J. R. R. *The Hobbit*. New York: Houghton Mifflin, 1988.

Travis, John W., and Regina Sara Ryan. *The Wellness Workbook*. Berkeley: Ten Speed Press, 1988.

Von Oech, Roger. *A Kick in the Seat of the Pants*. New York: Harper & Row, 1986.

Von Oech, Roger. *A Whack on the Side of the Head*. New York: Warner Books, 1983.

Williams, Margery. *The Velveteen Rabbit*. New York: Doubleday, 1969.

Witkin-Lanoil, Georgia. *The Female Stress Syndrome: How to Recognize and Live with It*. New York: Newmarket Press, 1984.

Wonder, Jacquelyn, and Priscilla Donovan. *Whole Brain Thinking: Working from Both Sides of the Brain to Achieve Peak Performance*. New York: Ballantine, 1983.

Zdenek, Marilee. *The Right-Brain Experience*. New York: McGraw-Hill, 1985.

Zundel, Stan L. *I Climb to Live: Health and Transcendance on the Mountain*. Los Angeles: Stan L. Zundel Publisher, 1979.

INDEX